Plant Organs

Q1 Below is shown a picture of a smiley plant. Label its four main organs.

1) ....

2) ....

3) ....

4) ....

Q2 Which of the plant's four main organs contains the reproductive organs?

....

Q3 Which of the plant's four main organs are the organs of photosynthesis?

....

Q4 The roots are important to a plant for several reasons. For example, they take up some of the substances needed for nutrition.

a) What are the two substances that a plant takes in through its roots for nutrition?

....

b) Name another reason why a plant has roots.

....

Q5 What do leaves contain that uses light to change carbon dioxide and water into glucose?

....

If you're stuck... see Page 2 of our KS3 Revision Guide (Levels 3-6)

Specialised Cells and Organs

Q1 This question is about sperm cells. Look at the picture below of a sperm cell.

a) What is the purpose of the sperm cell's tail?

....

....

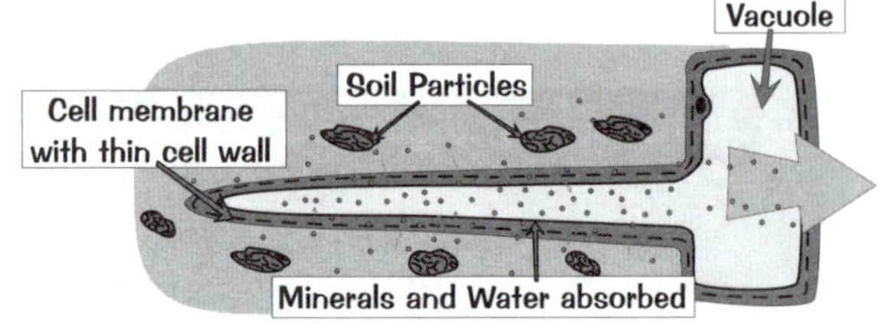

b) What is the name given to the type of information contained in the chromosomes?

....

c) What is the job of the enzymes that are carried in the head of the sperm cell?

....

....

....

Q2 This question is about root hair cells. Look at the picture below of this type of cell.

Name two things that the root hair cell absorbs for nutrition?

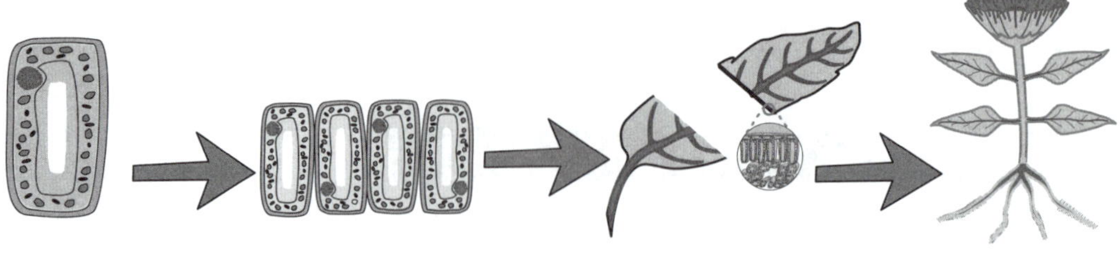

1) ....

2) ....

Q3 The following sequence shows how various bits come together to make an organism.

a) Label the sequence using the following words: organ, tissue, organism, cell.

....

b) Is it OK to use this sort of sequence for animals as well?

....

Contents

A few pages have got a splodge like this one where bits have been taken out of the syllabus. This stuff shouldn't come up in the SATs, but it's still really important so we left it in.

Life Processes and Cells

Q1 The seven life processes are things that all living organisms do.

Write down the seven life processes in the spaces below.

1) ....

2) ....

3) ....

4) ....

5) ....

6) ....

7) ....

Q2 Below is shown a picture of an animal cell. Label the three main parts of the cell.

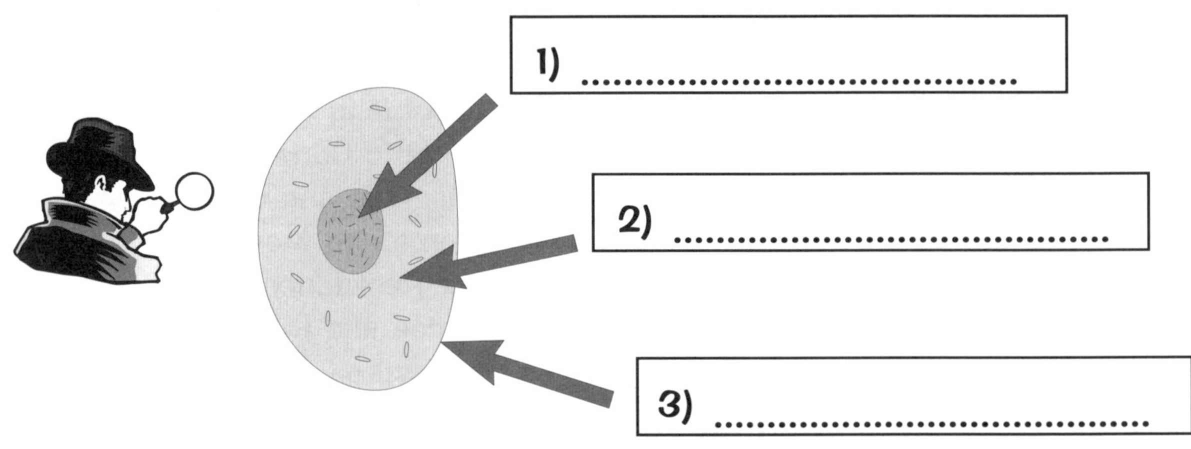

1) ....

2) ....

3) ....

Q3 A picture of a plant cell is shown below. Label the six main parts of the cell.

1) ....

4) ....

2) ....

5) ....

3) ....

6) ....

Human Organ System

Q1   Write the names of the nine major organ systems of the Human Body.

1) .... 6) ....

2) .... 7) ....

3) .... 8) ....

4) .... 9) ....

5) ....

Q2   Label the diagram below with the names of the five sense organs.

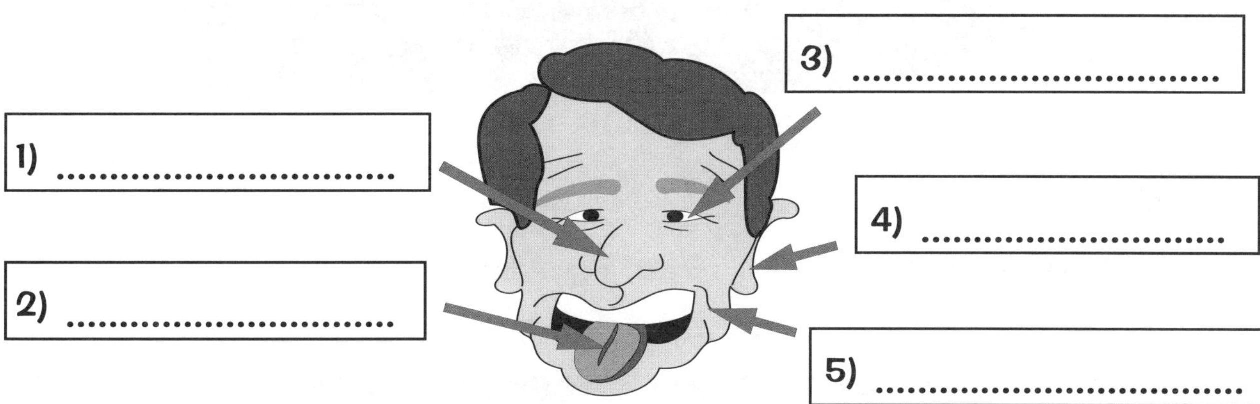

1) ....

2) ....

3) ....

4) ....

5) ....

Q3   Which organ system is responsible for taking in oxygen and removing carbon dioxide?

....

Q4   The skeleton has two main jobs.

a)   Name the two main jobs of the skeleton.

1) ....

2) ....

b)   What important job does the skull have to perform every time you bang your head?

....

....

If you're stuck… see Pages 4/5 of our KS3 Revision Guide (Levels 3-6) ☺

Nutrition

Q1 Name the seven food groups which are essential for healthy living.

1) ....

2) ....

3) ....

4) ....

5) ....

6) ....

7) ....

Q2 Which of the following food groups is the best source of protein? Circle the correct food group.

bread / potatoes / cereals   meat / eggs / fish   butter / cooking oil / cream

Q3 Blood, teeth, nerves and the thyroid gland are kept healthy by taking the right amount of which food group?

....

Q4 Why are carbohydrates important for the body?

....

....

....

Q5 Why is it important to drink lots of water?

....

....

....

<u>Digestion</u>

Q1 What is meant by the word "digestion"?

....

....

....

Q2 What are the two main steps in the process of digestion?

1) ....

2) ....

Q3 In the diagram below, label the six main parts of the digestive system.

....

....

....

....

....

....

If you're stuck... see Page 8 of our KS3 Revision Guide (Levels 3-6) ☺

Absorption in the Gut

Q1 Complete the following sentences about absorption by circling the correct words.

Enzymes are used to _break up_ / _combine_ big molecules so that small ones can be made. These smaller molecules _cannot_ / _can_ pass through the gut wall into the blood. They then pass _into_ / _out of_ the cells and are used by the body.

Q2 On the diagram below, label the names of the three different types of enzyme the body uses to help it absorb food.

Starch   →   Glucose and other simple sugars

Protein   →   Amino acids

Fats   →   Glycerol Fatty Acids

Q3 In which part of the digestive system is food absorbed?

Q4 In which part of the digestive system is water absorbed?

Q5 The small intestine is covered with millions of villi. What are villi and what is their job?

The Circulatory System

Q1 Complete the sentences below about the circulatory system. Fill in the gaps correctly using the words from the grey box.

> oxygen   4   oxygenated   deoxygenated   heart
> pumped   2   3   oxygen   1

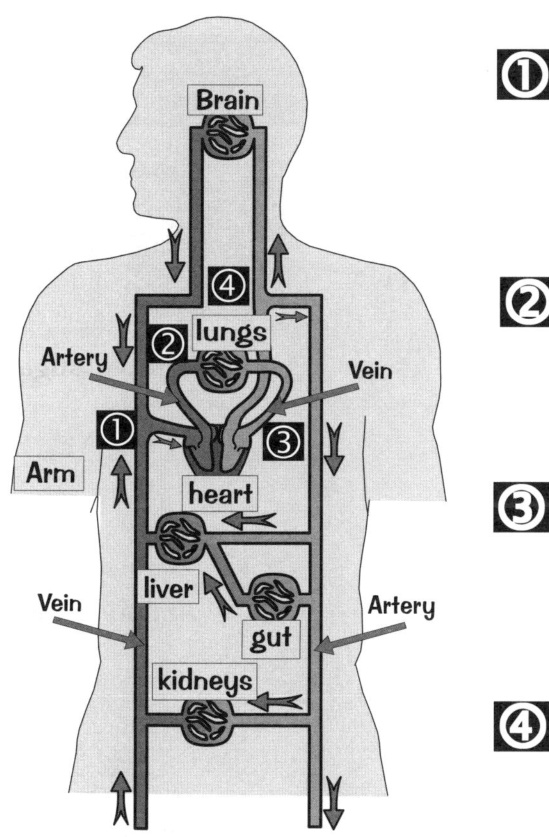

① ....
blood enters the heart

② It's then pumped to the lungs to pick
up some ....

③ It's now ....
and travels back to the ....

④ It's then .... around
the body so every cell gets the vital
.... that it needs.

The sequence then *repeats*

from step number ......

Q2 Label the following blood vessels correctly using the following words:
Arteries, capillaries, veins.

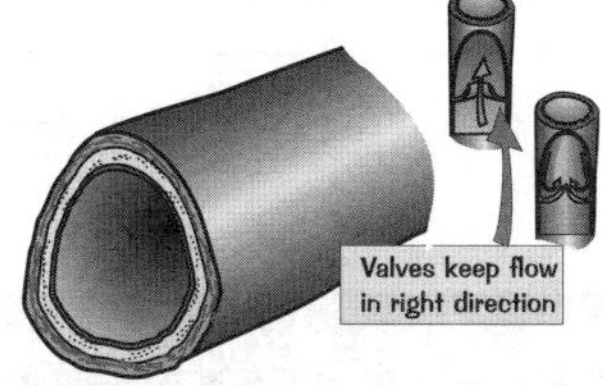

These have thin walls
which help food particles
etc. to pass through.

These carry blood at low
pressure back to the heart.

These carry blood at
high pressure away
from the heart.

....

Skeleton, Joints and Muscles

Q1 What are the three key functions of the human skeleton?

1) ....

2) ....

3) ....

Q2 Look at the diagram of the Human Skeleton.

a) What is the job of the backbone?

....

....

....

b) What is the job of the rib cage?

....

....

....

Q3 Draw arrows to match up these examples of bones to the correct descriptions.

| immovable | slightly movable | freely movable |

Q4 Complete the following sentences about muscles by circling the correct words.

Muscles work in _pairs_ / _trios_ against each other. One muscle contracts while the other _two_ / _one_ relaxes (lengthens), and vice versa. _Tendons_ / _ligaments_ attach the muscles to the bones. One _muscle_ / _cockle_ pulls the bone in one direction and the other pulls it in the _opposite_ / _same_ direction.

Growing Up

Q1 Label the following diagram of the Human male reproductive system.

Tube from the ....

....

....

....

....

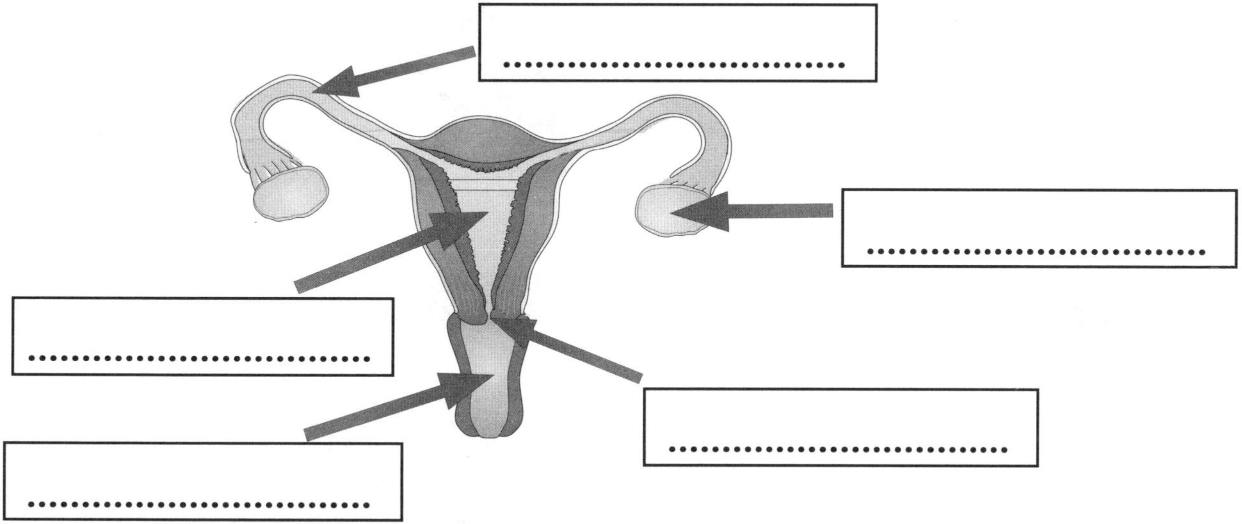

Q2 Label the following diagram of the Human female reproductive system.

....

....

....

....

....

Q3 The female menstrual cycle is a 28 day cycle. Read the descriptions below and write down whether they occur on the 1st, 4th, 14th or 28th day of the cycle.

Day Number

The _lining_ of the uterus starts to build up again.   ....

The wall remains thick awaiting the arrival of a
fertilised egg.   ....

An egg is released from the ovaries of the female.   ....

Bleeding starts as the lining of the uterus (the
womb) breaks down and passes out of the vagina.   ....

      If you're stuck... see Pages 12/13 of our KS3 Revision Guide (Levels 3-6) ☺

Having a Baby

Q1 Fill in the missing labels.

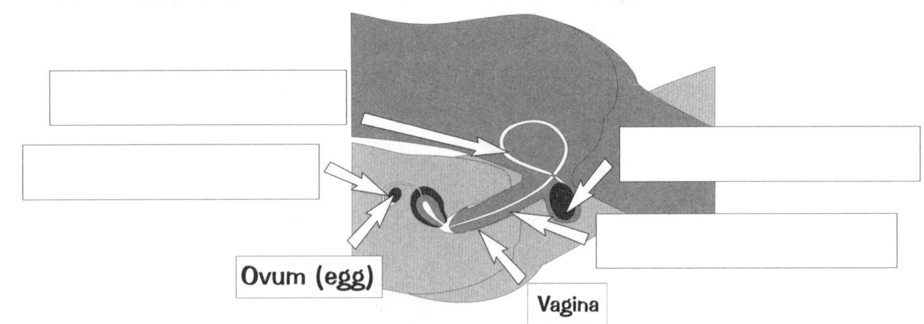

Q2 Put the following stages of fertilisation in the correct order.

cell division, ovulation, implantation, fertilisation, copulation

1 ....

2 ....

3 ....

4 ....

5 ....

Q3 Complete the following diagram using the words provided.

Embryo

Mother's blood

Umbilical cord

Placenta

Amnion (bag)

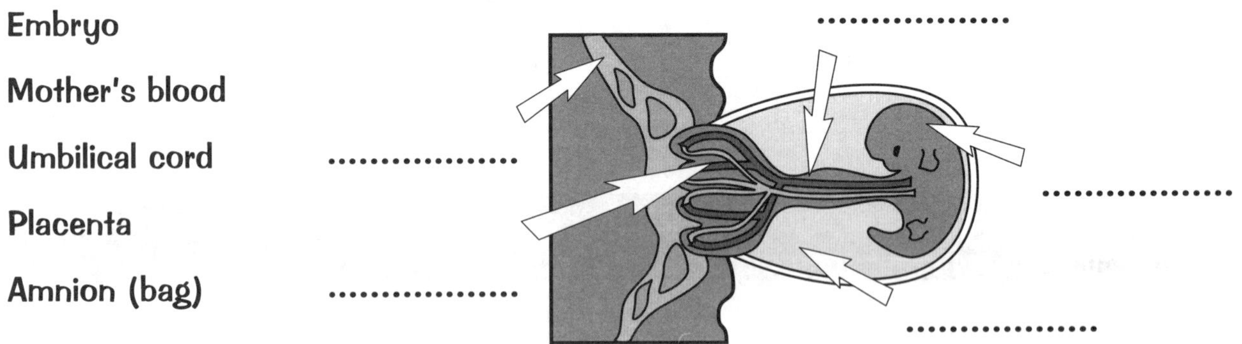

Q4 At what time after conception do the following developments occur?

.... month(s)   .... month(s)   .... month(s)   .... month(s)

The embryo has a brain, heart, eyes and legs.

It kicks and it's pesky finger nails can be felt.

The foetus is viable.

The baby is fully developed

Breathing

Q1 Label the diagram below using words from the list on the right.

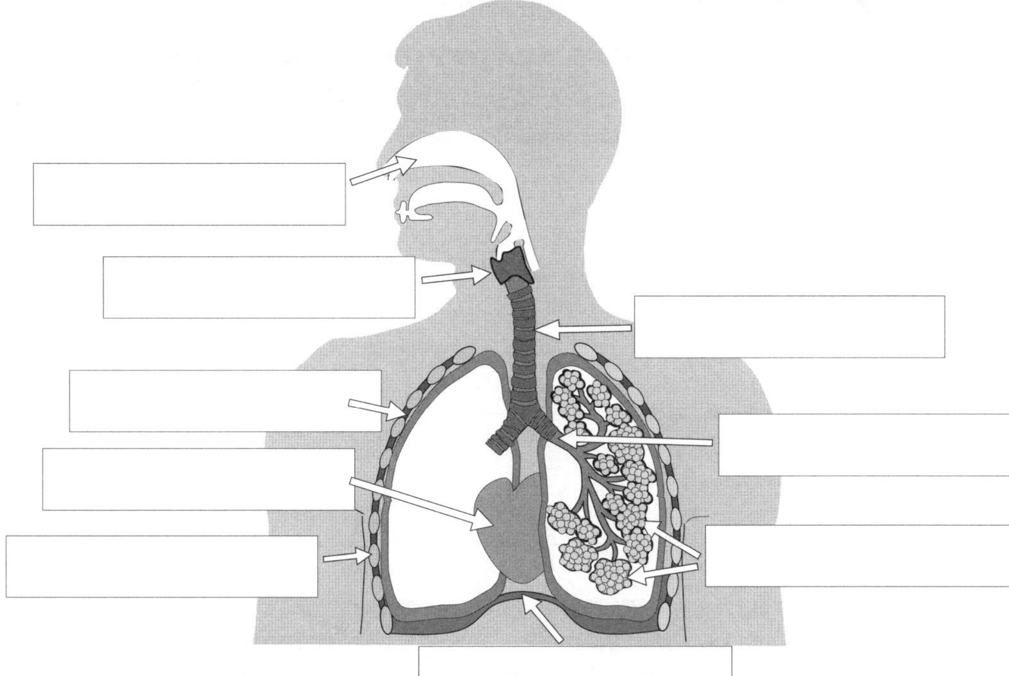

Q2 Use the following words to fill in the spaces:

blood,   lungs,   breathing,   oxygen,   air,   carbon dioxide,   energy.

The _______________ we need to stay alive comes from the ___________

which enters our _________________.

The waste gases, ___________ _______________ and water vapour

leave our body and the whole process is called _______________.

The important gas we take in is absorbed into our _________________ and

is used with sugar in the cells to give us _________________________.

Q3 Describe the process of a) breathing in, and b) breathing out.
Use the diagrams to help you.

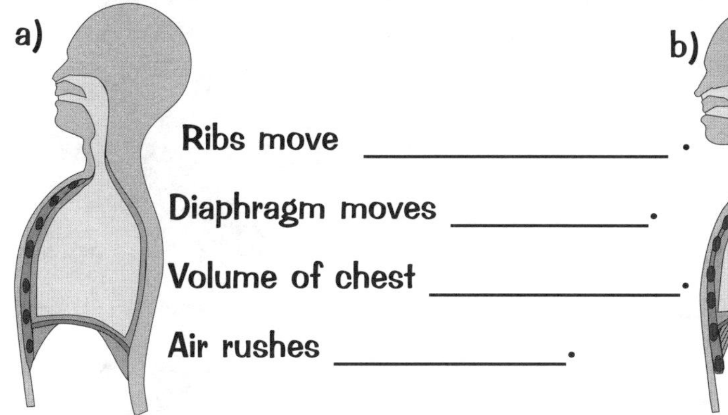

Smoking

Q1 The apparatus below has been set up to represent what happens to a person's lungs when they smoke a cigarette.

Explain what will happen to a) the temperature and b) the glass wool when the cigarette smoke is sucked through the glass tubing.

....

....

....

....

....

Q2 Complete the table below showing the three types of grot smoking puts in our lungs.

Type of Grot	What the Grot does to the body
....	Is an addictive drug that raises the heart beat rate, narrows the arteries and causes high blood pressure. This leads to **HEART DISEASE.**
Tar	....
....	This is a <u>poisonous gas</u> which joins up with red blood cells making them incapable of transporting **OXYGEN** around the body.

Q3 List five of the bad effects that smoking has on your body.

1 ....

2 ....

3 ....

4 ....

5 ....

<u>Respiration</u>

Q1 Complete the word equation for respiration.
The first letter of each word has already been put in.

G........ + O........ = C........ d........ + W...... | + E........

Q2 The experiment below shows a girl blowing into a tube. The tube goes through a trough of iced water and then into a beaker containing limewater.

After breathing into the tube, water residue was found in the U-tube and the limewater had gone cloudy.

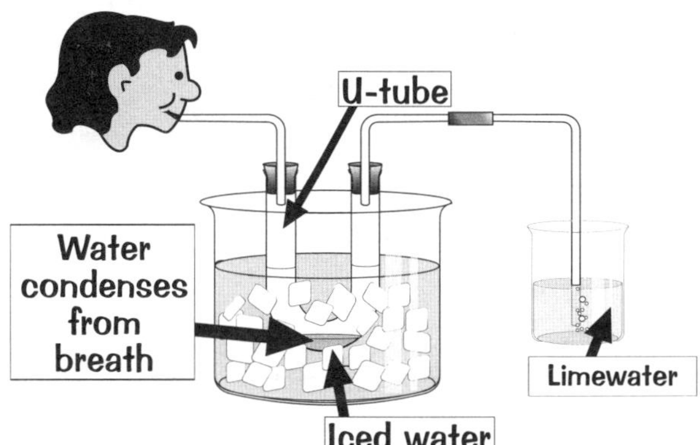

Explain why:
a) there was water residue in the U-tube
b) the limewater was cloudy.

a) ....

....

b) ....

....

Q3 The energy created from respiration is used by the body in many ways.
Use the graphics beneath to help you remember six of them.

1 ....

2 ....

3 ....

4 ....

5 ....

6 ....

Health

Q1   Having a healthy body means several things. Fill in the blanks in the list below.

a) The absence of ....

b) Eating a balanced ....

c) Doing enough ....

d) Not abusing ....

Q2   Complete the following paragraph adding words from the word lists given.

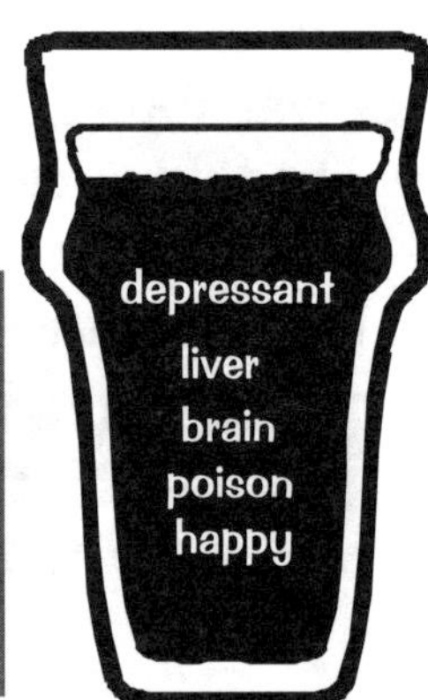

Alcohol is a ...., despite the fact that it may give a .... feeling.
It's a .... which affects the ....
and .... leading to various health problems.

lungs, character, brain, liver, mind, kidneys, behaviour

Solvents are drugs because they cause hallucinations, which are illusions of the .... Solvents can have psychological effects on the .... and .... of the abuser.
They also cause serious damage to the ...., the
.........................., ... and ....

Q3   Match the illegal drug to the effects they cause.

Hallucinogens

> Examples: Heroin and Morphine. They are extremely addictive and can both cause severe degeneration of a person's life.

Pain Killers

> Examples: Ecatasy and LSD. Ecstasy can give the feeling of boundless energy which can lead to overheating, dehydration and sometimes DEATH.

Stimulants

> Example: Barbiturates. They slow down a persons body which can be dangerous. They can help sleeping but they're seriously habit-forming.

Depressants

> Examples: Amphetamine (speed) and Methedrine. They give a feeling of boundless energy, they're addictive so behaviour and personality change.

Fighting Disease

Q1 Fill in the gaps. All the words you need are in the grey box.

> immune, medicines, white, blood, cells, natural,
> immunisation, antibodies, defences

The body has its own .... against disease but it can be helped by .... and .... The main armies of defence of the body are .... and .... which are part of the body's .... system.

Q2 Do antibiotics work on bacteria, viruses or both? ....

Q3 Give two examples of bacterial diseases and two examples of viral diseases.

Bacteria .... 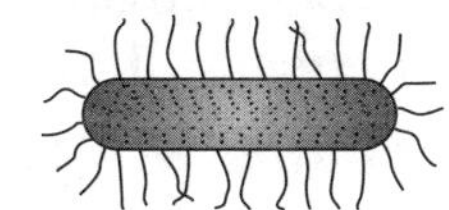   Viruses ....

.... 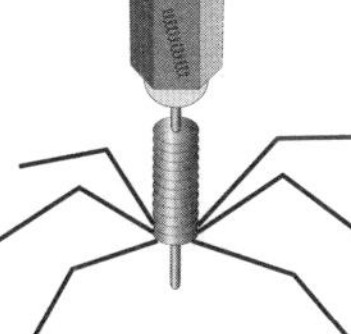

Q4 Find and circle the nine underlined words from the text.

"White blood cells attack microbes in three ways. Firstly they gobble them up whole. Secondly they produce antibodies to neutralise and prepare microbes for gobbling. Lastly they neutralise any poisons or toxins produced by the microbes. Once the white blood cells recognise a microbe they can act immediately to stop you getting ill. This is called immunity"

M	G	N	I	K	O	M	S	E	V	I	E	W
D	I	I	J	B	C	I	L	I	A	T	S	H
E	B	C	E	L	L	S	E	Z	N	B	I	I
C	S	R	R	O	N	M	O	N	O	X	L	T
S	E	I	D	O	B	I	T	N	A	S	A	E
M	S	W	L	D	B	P	I	P	N	G	R	P
Q	I	J	D	A	C	E	A	O	Q	O	T	L
S	L	R	O	N	C	H	S	O	L	E	U	U
N	Y	P	E	T	T	I	I	N	H	A	E	O
I	J	V	R	U	O	M	U	T	E	G	N	D
X	N	J	D	P	B	L	A	R	I	O	E	C
O	M	R	F	Y	T	I	N	U	M	M	I	C
T	M	R	F	W	T	M	U	C	U	S	C	C

If you're stuck... see Page 19 of our KS3 Revision Guide (Levels 3-6) ☺

How Plants Make Food

Q1 What do plants use photosynthesis to make? ....

Q2 Use the words from the word list to complete the photosynthesis equation.

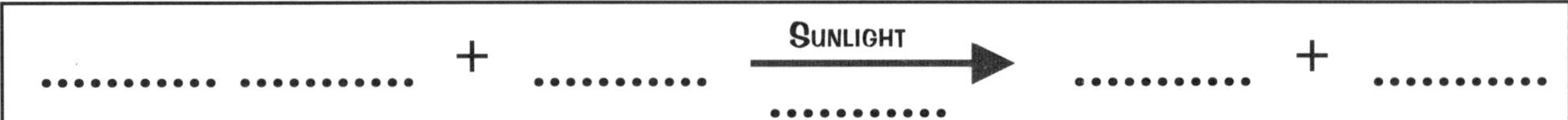

Oxygen, Water, Glucose, Carbon dioxide, Chlorophyll

.... + ... $\xrightarrow{\text{SUNLIGHT}}$ .... + ...
....

Q3 Fill in the blanks. Each word is something plants need for photosynthesis.

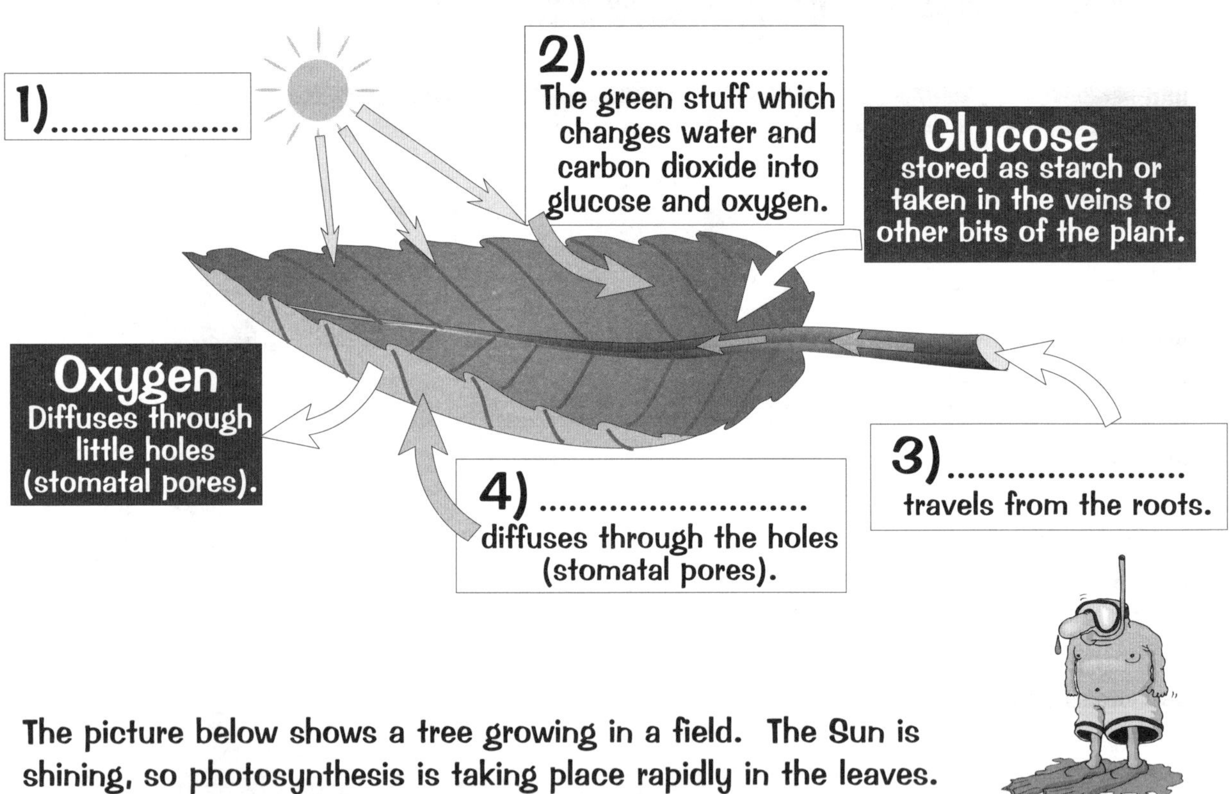

Q4 The picture below shows a tree growing in a field. The Sun is shining, so photosynthesis is taking place rapidly in the leaves.

a) What substance is _taken in_ from the air by the tree? ....

b) What substance is _given out_ into the air by the tree? ....

c) What substance needed for photosynthesis does the tree take from the soil?

....

Photosynthesis

Q1 Iodine can be used to test for starch in leaves. When tested, the leaves from a plant that had been kept in the dark for 24 hours went brown. The leaves from a plant that had been kept in the light for 24 hours went black.

Why had starch been produced in the second plant and not the first?

....

Q2 Complete this crossword about photosynthesis.

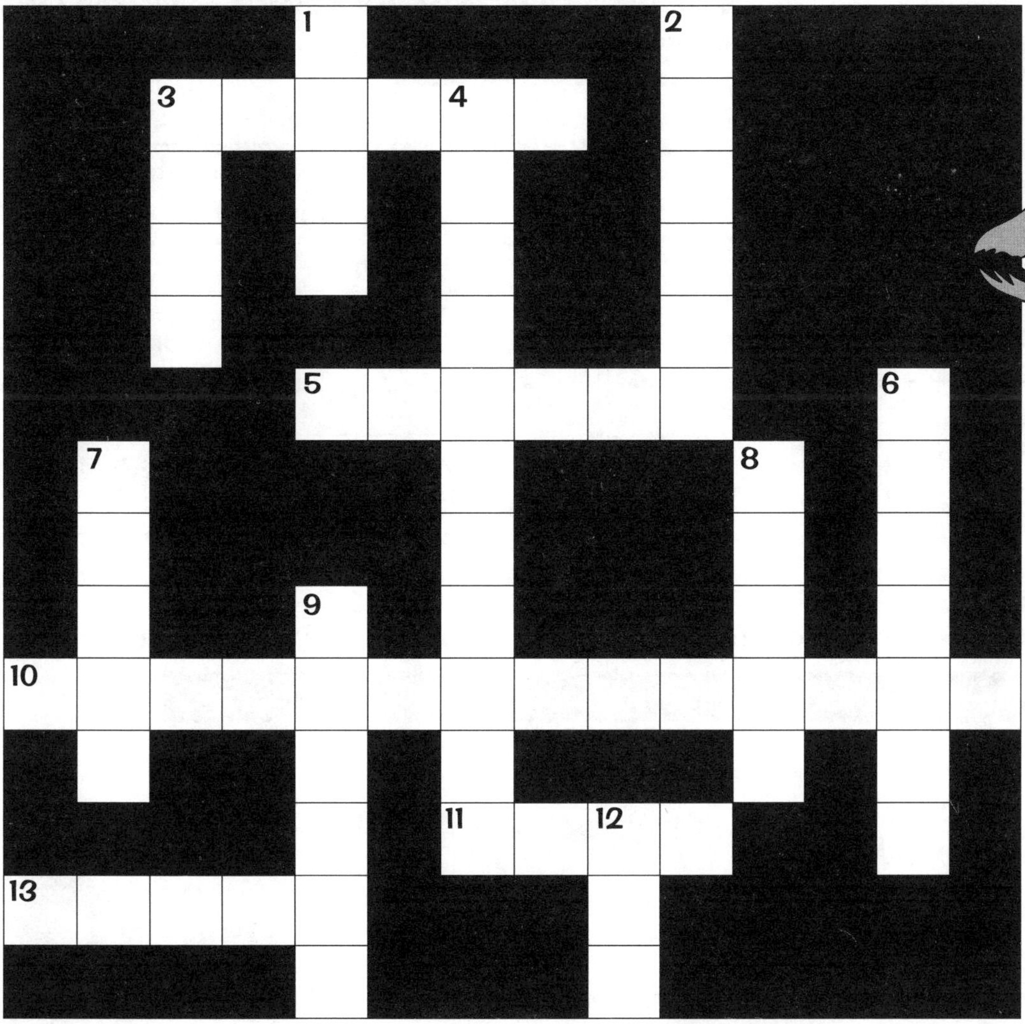

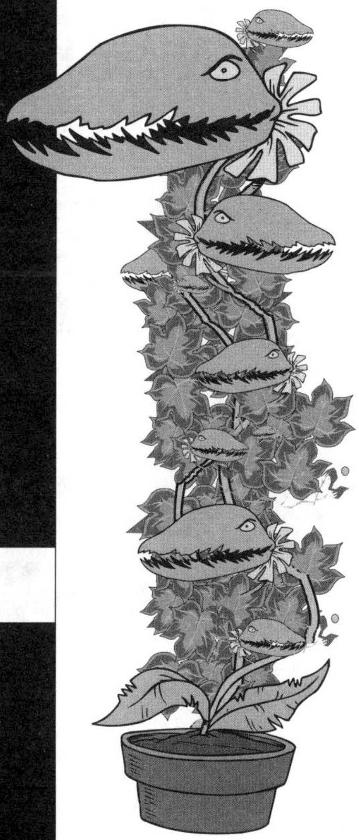

Across

3) Sugars are stored as this (6).
5) across and **6)** down — gas needed for photosynthesis (6,7)
10) How plants make food (14)
11) Food is made here (4)
13) Chlorophyll looks like this (5)

Down

1) Plants can't photosynthesise in this (4)
2) We need it — plants make it in the light (6)
3) Roots get water from here (4)
4) Pigment that absorbs light (11)
6) see 5) across
7) Energy needed to make sugars (5)
8) Liquid needed for photosynthesis (5)
9) Test for starch with this solution (6)
12) Carbon dioxide comes from here (3)

Plant Growth

Q1 Give two special features that make root hairs good at absorption.

1 ....

2 ....

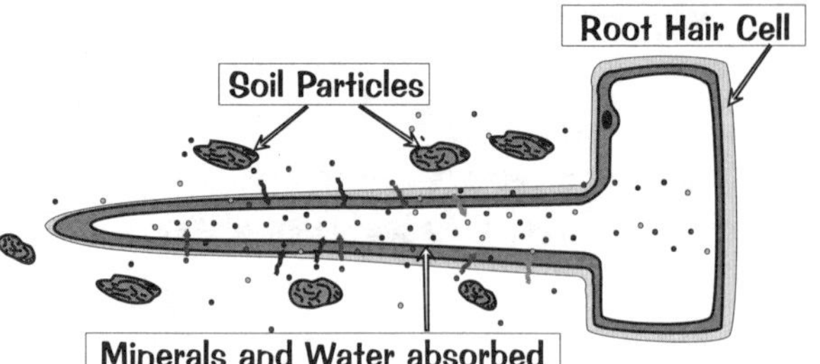

Q2 Nitrates, phosphates and potassium are the three essential minerals needed by plants.
Match up the essential minerals with what they do.

Nitrates	Provide phosphorous which is needed for photosynthesis and respiration.
Phosphates	Helps enzymes to work properly.
Potassium	Provide nitrogen which is needed for making proteins.

Q3 Plants show specific symptoms if they are missing one of the essential minerals.
Complete the sentences below that say what each plant is missing.

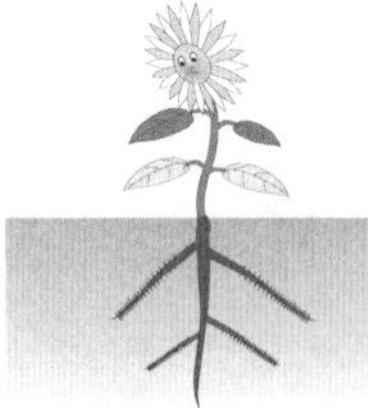

A *small* plant with *yellow* older leaves.

This plant is lacking ....

Poor root growth and *purple* younger leaves.

This plant is lacking ....

Yellow leaves with *dead bits*.

This plant is lacking ....

Plant Reproduction

Q1 Use the words from the word list to label the parts of the flower shown below.

anther, filament, petals, stigma, style, ovary, sepals

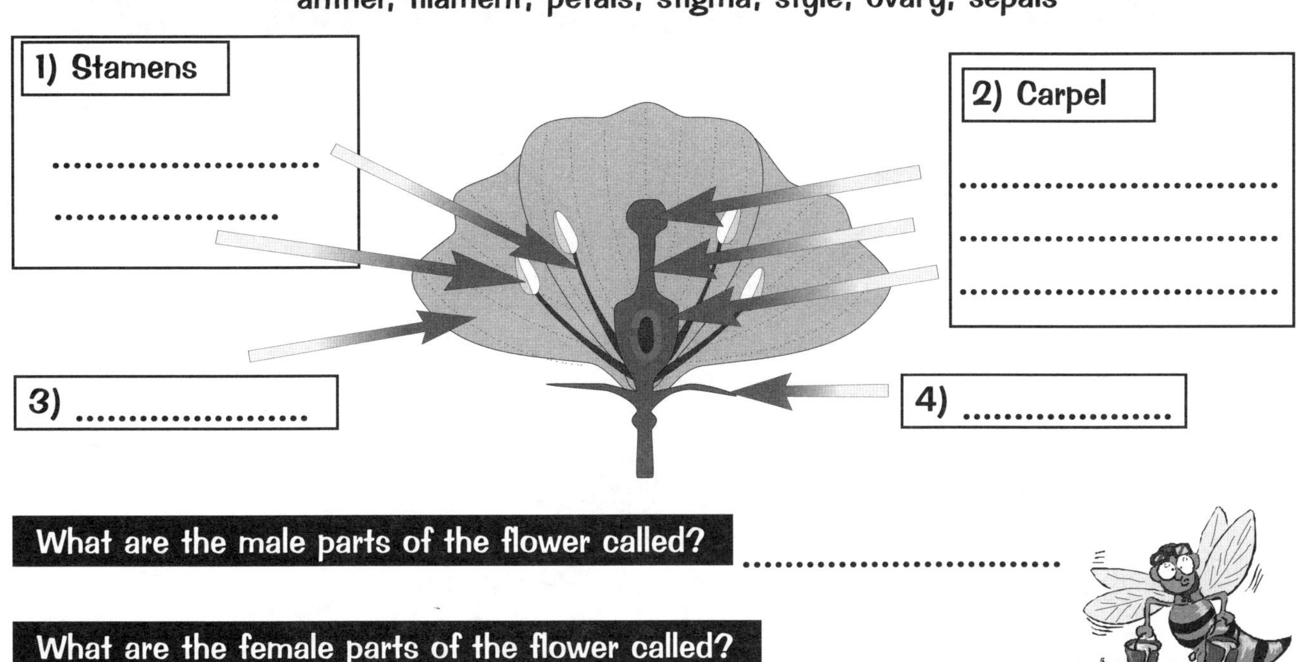

Q2 What are the male parts of the flower called?   ....

Q3 What are the female parts of the flower called?   ....

Q4 Complete the sentences by joining a beginning with an ending with an arrow:

Beginnings → Endings

Beginnings	Endings
the female sex cell in plants is called	the filament and anther
the female sex organ in plants is called	the stigma, style and ovary
the female sex organ is made up from	the carpel
the male sex cell in plants is called	the stamen
the male sex organ in plants is called	the pollen
the male sex organ is made up from	the ova

Q5 Write down the differences between these two flowers and say whether they are wind or insect pollinated.

....
....
....
....
....

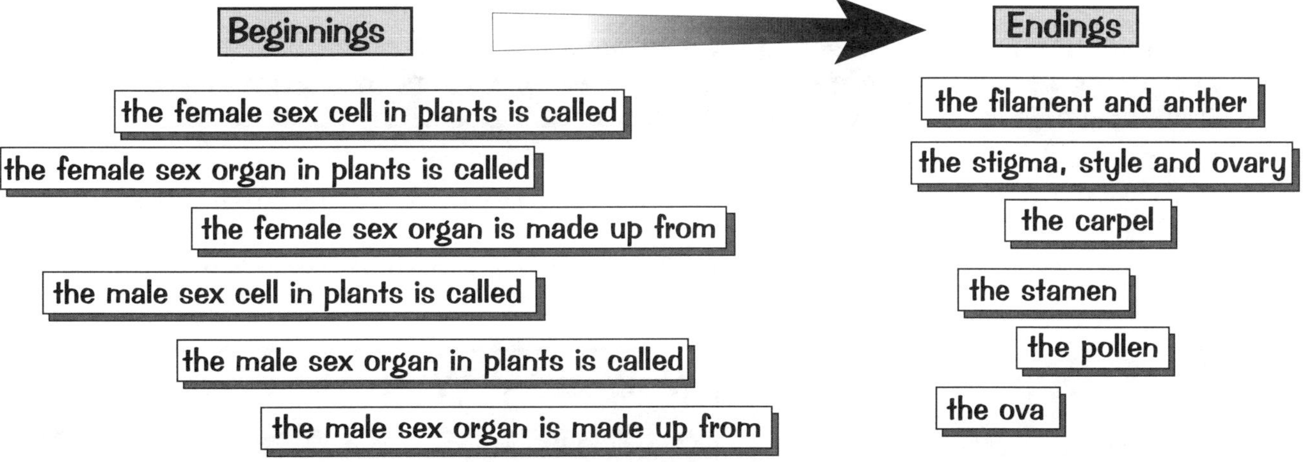

Plant Reproduction and Seeds

Q1   Plants disperse their seeds in a number of ways.

Write down whether the following are dispersed by the wind, animals or explosively.

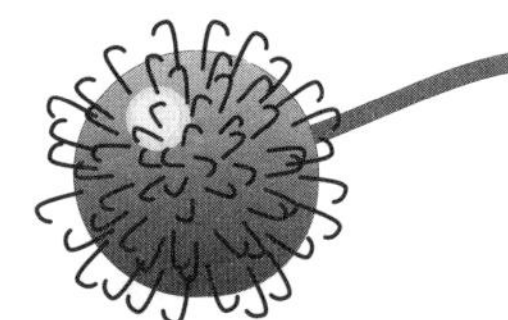

Burdock fruit
(has tiny hooks)

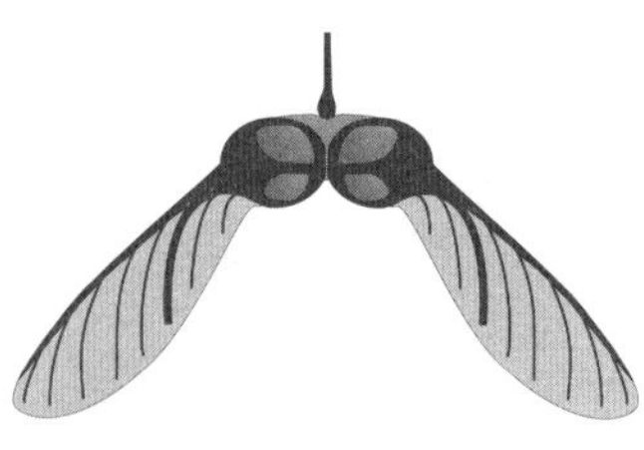

Sycamore fruit

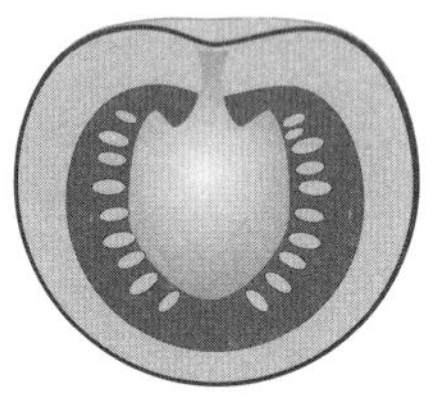

Tomato fruit

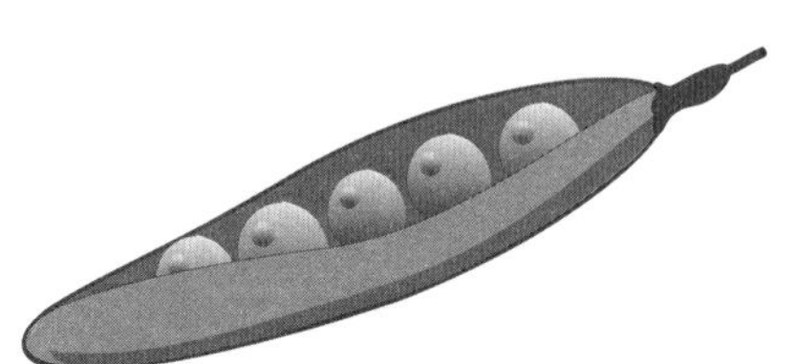

Peas in a pod

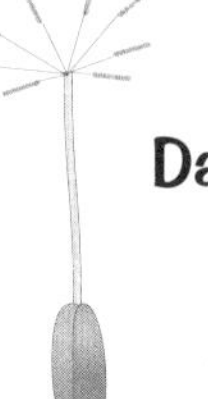

Dandelion fruit

Wind dispersed: ....

Dispersed by animals: ....

Dispersed by explosion: ....

Q2   Germination is when the seeds start to grow.

What three conditions need to be just right for germination to happen?

....

....

Q3   **Have a go at the flower wordsearch.**

The words to find are:

anther, filament, ovary, ovule, pollen, stigma, style.

There are two other words in the grid to do with flowers — can you find them both?

Here's a clue..

S _ _ _ _ _ N
C _ _ _ _ L

```
W P A O V U L E R A
C Z N T E B Z E M O
A E T N I H E G V G
R Y H E U U I I D S
P R E M Z T K E X P
E A R A S Q X A S O
L V F L D F N T S L
N O K I C O Y O L L
H P A F Q L D N P E
S T A M E N Y Y B N
```

The Carbon Cycle

Q1 Carbon is an important element because it is found in all living things. It's constantly recycled through the environment in the carbon cycle. The scene below shows some important steps in this cycle.

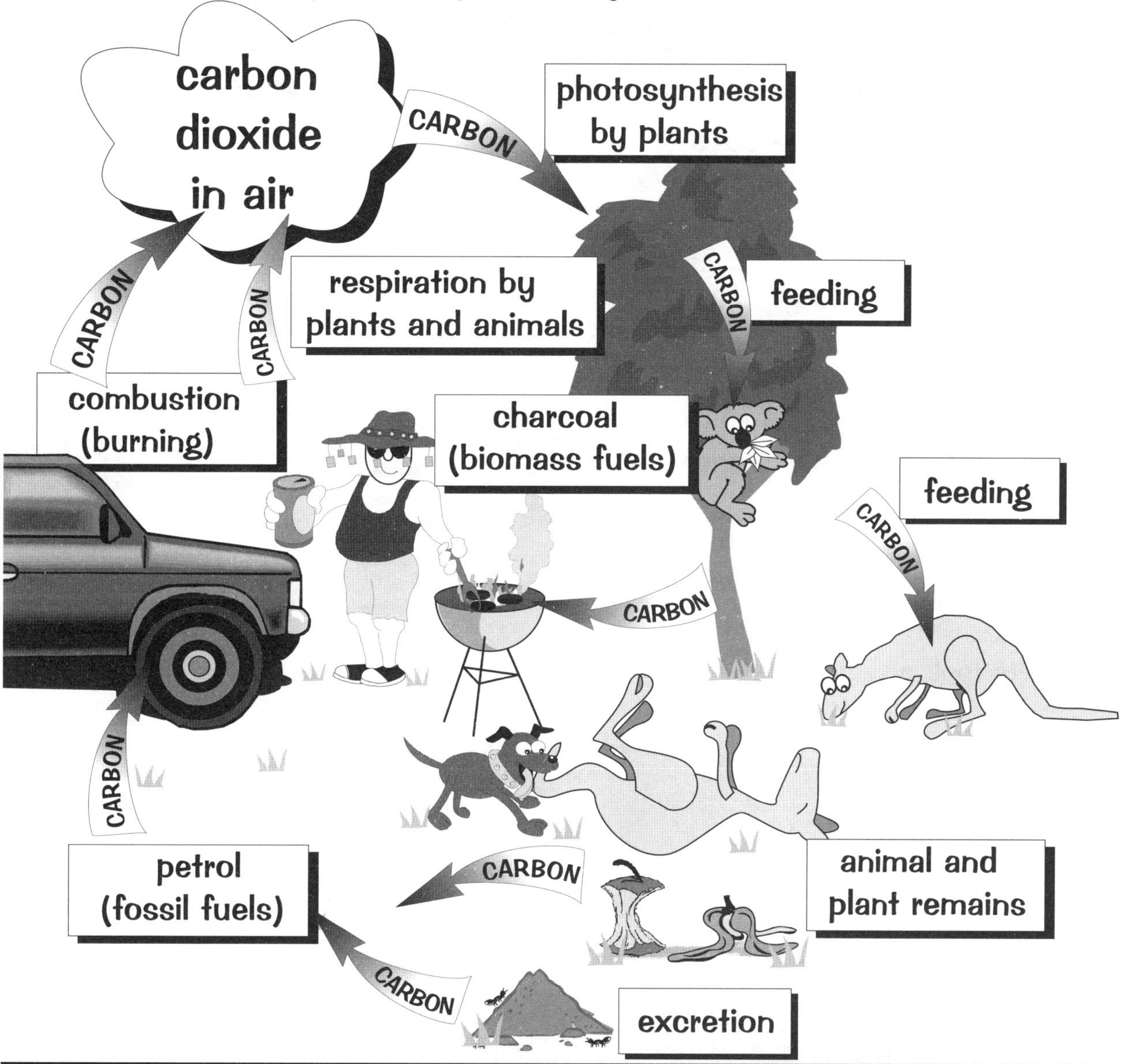

a) Which two processes in the picture contribute to the carbon dioxide in the air?

....

b) Plants take in carbon dioxide through photosynthesis. How does the carbon then get into animals?

....

c) Where does the carbon found in fossil fuels come from?

....

....

If you're stuck... see Page 26 of our KS3 Revision Guide (Levels 3-6) ☺

Inherited and Environmental Variation

Q1 Animals and plants do not all look the same, they vary. Some of this variation is inherited from their parents, and some is caused by the environment (where a plant grows, how you are brought up and what you eat, for example).

> Look at the picture of Jane below and put a tick next to each of her characteristics which have been inherited from her parents.

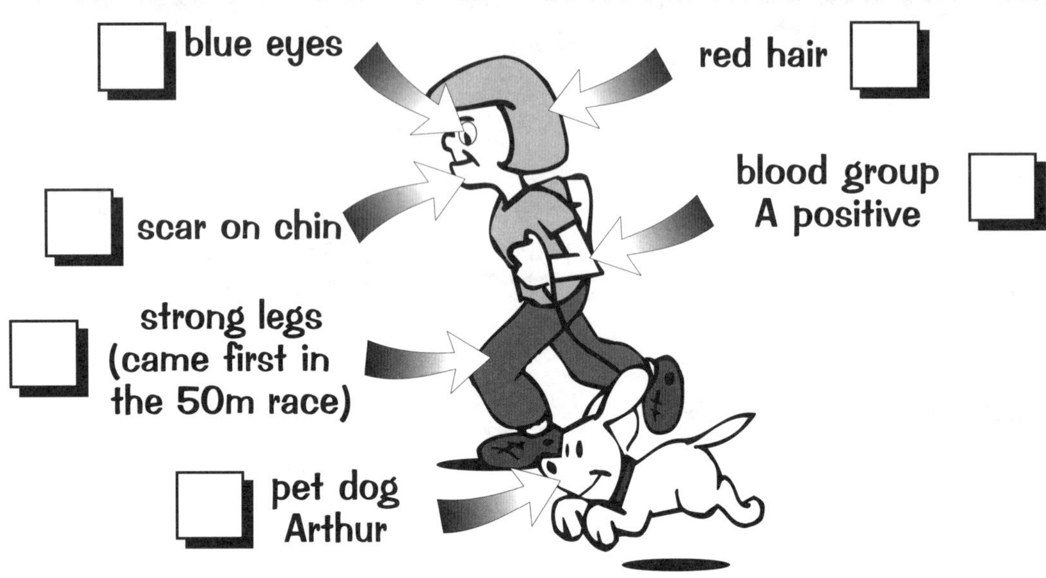

Q2 Mike took a seed from his dad's enormous sunflower plant in the greenhouse. He planted it in a pot in the garden expecting it to grow as big as him but after a month it was only half his size.

a) Are the differences between the plants due to inherited or environmental variation?

....

....

b) What are the four factors which might have affected his plant's growth?

....

....

c) What could Mike do to make his plant grow better?

....

....

....

Classification 

Q1 Look at the animals below and put a tick next to all of the vertebrates (those with a backbone) and a cross next to the invertebrates (those without a backbone).

shark □ snake □ slug □

butterfly □ tortoise □ dog □

Q2 Sarah saw some creatures in and around the pond in her garden. Classify each one as either insect, fish, amphibian or mollusc.

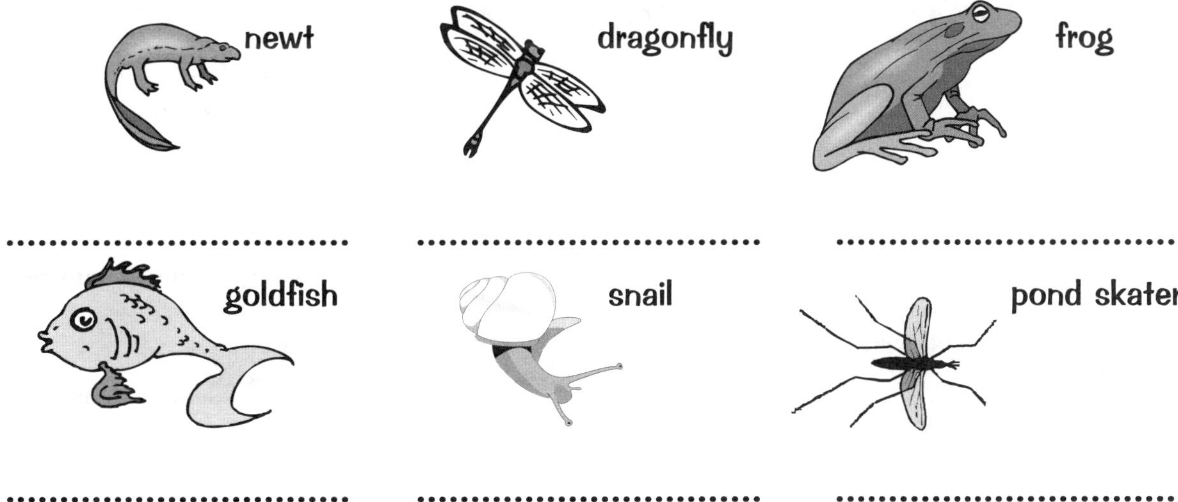

newt dragonfly frog

....

goldfish snail pond skater

....

Q3 Choose words from below to fill in the sentences about birds and mammals.

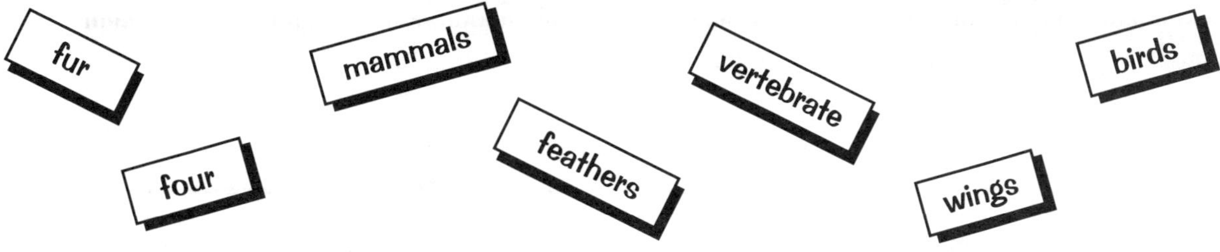

Birds and mammals have backbones and so belong to the ______________ group of animals.

Birds have ______________, ______________ and a beak while mammals have ______________

or hair and ______________ limbs.

______________ give birth to live young unlike ______________ which lay eggs.

Using Keys

Q1 Four aliens were found in a crater on the Moon. Use the key from the alien identification manual to classify them and write their names in the spaces.

A   B   C   D

....

....

1) Does the alien have flight appendages (wings)?

        YES .... go to question 2)

        NO .... go to question 3)

2) Does it have arms for grabbing scared astronauts?

        YES .... alien is a **GRABBING FLAPPOID**

        NO .... alien is an **ARMLESS FLAPPOID**

3) Does it have antennae for picking up radio signals from Earth?

        YES .... alien is an **EASY LISTENOID**

        NO .... alien is a **STANDARD MOONOID**

Q2 Use the key below to identify these four prehistoric characters.

1) Does it have four legs?   YES .... go to question 2

                                        NO .... go to question 3

2) Does it have pointy bits on its head?   YES .... it is a **TRICERATOPS**

                                        NO .... it is a **DIPLODOCUS**

3) Does it have a club and say 'ugh' a lot?   YES .... it is a **CAVEMAN**

                                        NO .... it is a **PTERODACTYL**

Adaptation

Q1 Polar bears are adapted to live in a very cold habitat. Fill in the blanks in the paragraph below with these words:

arctic   heat loss   fat   warm   rounded

Polar bears have special features to help them live in _________________ conditions. They have a thick layer of _______________ and a thick fur coat to keep them ______________. Their ________________ shape gives them a small surface area to reduce __________________.

Q2 Complete the sentences about the adaptations the camel has for living in the desert using the words below.

feet   store   drink   sand   fat   hump

Camels can _____________ and _____________ lots of water which is handy for those long dry spells.

_____________ is stored in its _____________ to assist the loss of heat from the rest of its body.

Big, wide _____________ stop it from sinking in the soft ___________.

If you're stuck... see Page 34 of our KS3 Revision Guide (Levels 3-6) ☺

Food Chains

Q1 Here is a food chain you might find in your own garden.

Leaf → Worm → Bird → Cat

a) What do the arrows mean in food chains?

....

b) Name an animal from the food chain which is a herbivore.

....

c) Which animal is a carnivore?

....

Q2 Draw lines to connect the words on the left with their correct meanings.

carnivores — animals that can eat both plants and animals

omnivores — animals that eat plants

herbivores — animals that eat other animals

consumers — organisms that can make their own food

producers — organisms that rely on other organisms for their food

Q3 The names below are all words to do with food chains, but with the letters muddled up. Unscramble the letters to find out what the words are and then find them in the word search. The first one has been done for you:

Vince Roar, Mrs Oncue, Dina Choof, Ron Movie, Dr Prouce, Rover Hibe.

carnivore ....

....

....

....

....

....

E	P	C	O	N	S	U	M	E	R
R	R	F	O	I	D	C	H	A	O
O	E	O	O	A	E	R	B	M	I
V	C	O	M	H	I	V	N	C	A
I	U	D	A	C	H	I	N	G	R
B	D	C	E	D	V	O	R	E	S
R	O	H	S	O	K	I	Z	X	L
E	R	A	R	O	A	R	N	I	V
H	P	E	R	F	V	I	B	R	A
X	E	R	O	V	I	N	R	A	C

Food Webs

Q1   Below is a food web found in rivers and waterways.

a) Fill in the letters missing in each word.

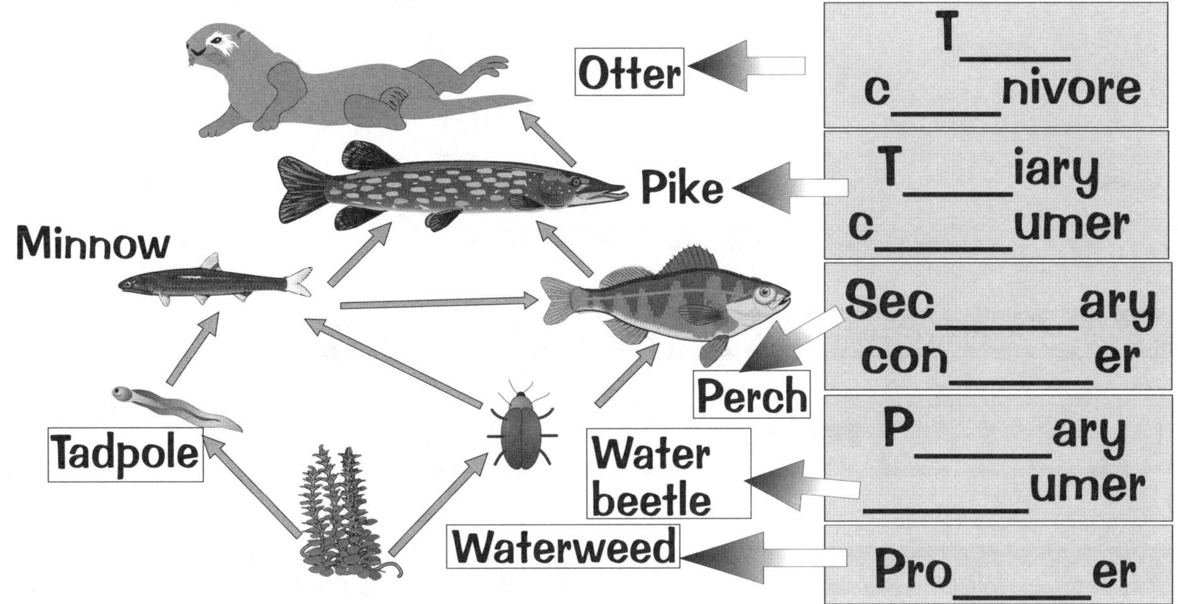

b) Which of these animals are herbivores?

....

....

c) Which of these animals are carnivores?

....

....

....

....

d) What do minnows eat?

....

....

e) A fisherman came and caught all of the perch. Circle the correct answer in these questions about what will happen in the foodweb.

There will be   _more_ / _less_   water beetles so the water weed will be eaten   _more_ / _less_.

The minnows will have   _more_ / _less_   food but will be eaten   _more_ / _less_   by the pike.

Problems in Food Chains

Q1 Look at the pyramid of numbers below and answer the following questions.

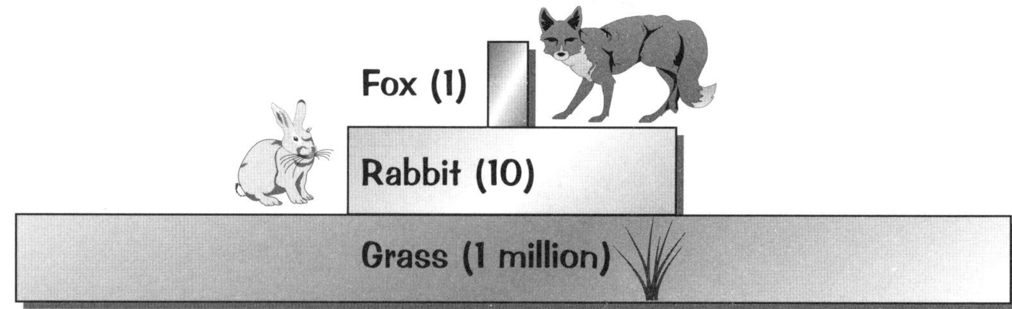

a) Complete this food chain with the organisms from above.

☐ → ☐ → ☐

b) What information does the pyramid give us about each level in the food chain?

....

....

....

c) The grass is growing in a field which has been sprayed with pesticide. What will happen to the level of pesticide as it is passed along the food chain?

....

....

Q2 Draw a pyramid of numbers for the food chain below and next to it draw an arrow showing the direction in which energy is passed.

oak tree (1) → caterpillar (100) → blue tit (10)

energy is passed
this way

Survival 

Q1 Look at these three lobsters and answer the questions below:

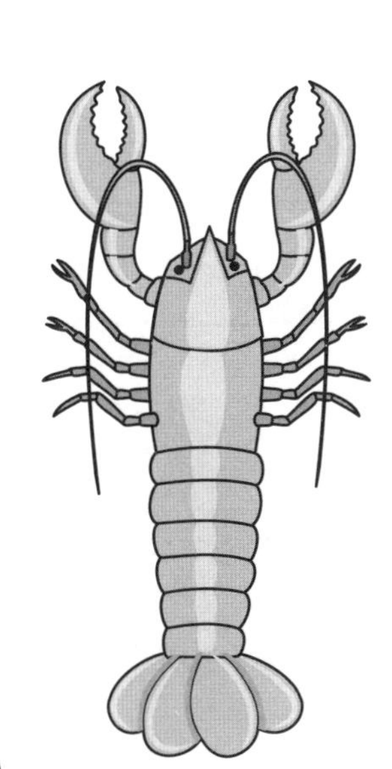

A

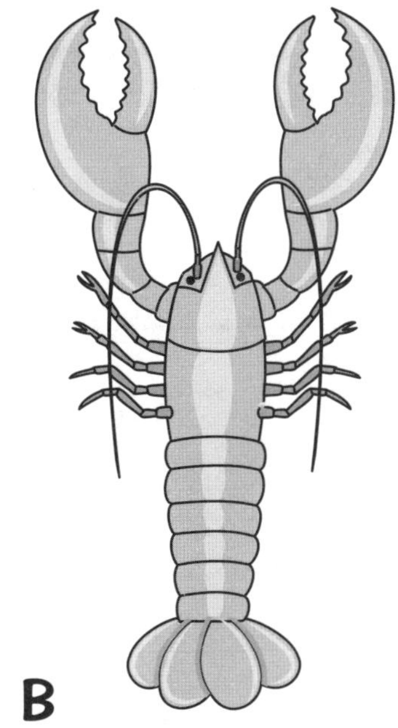

B

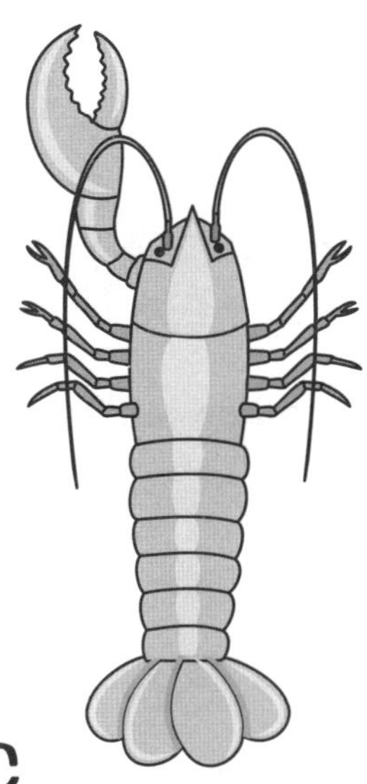

C

a) What adaptation do lobsters use to catch their prey and protect themselves?

....

b) In a population of lobsters which lobster would be most likely to survive? Why?

....

....

....

c) Use these words to finish the paragraph below.

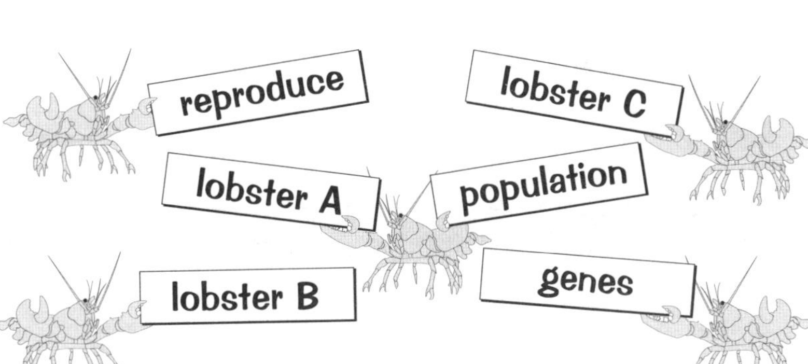

In a population of lobsters the individuals which are most like ______________

would survive best. This means that they are more likely to ______________

and pass their ______________ on to their young. Gradually the whole

population would become more and more like ______________ .

If you're stuck... see Page 38 of our KS3 Revision Guide (Levels 3-6) ☺

Types of Material 

Q1 Five different materials are listed below. Under each material is an example of one of its uses.

Explain why that material is well suited to its use.

a) Metal (making car, van bodies etc.)

....
....

b) Plastic (plugs and wire insulation)

....
....

c) Glass (lightbulbs)

....
....

d) Fibres (clothes)

....
....

e) Ceramics (bricks)

....
....

Q2 **Some of the above materials are recyclable. What does this mean?**

....
....
....

Q3 Reinforced concrete is made out of concrete with steel bars running through it. **Why do you think this gives it so much strength?**

....
....

Materials and their Properties

Q1 A list of words describing the various properties of some materials is given below.

List three useful properties of the material used to make the window pane and the girder. Some properties are given below to help you.

conductor of electricity   magnetic
flexible   hard   brittle   insulator of electricity
malleable
strong   transparent   insulator of heat
conductor of heat   translucent

window pane

a ....

b ....

c ....

steel girder

d ....

e ....

f ....

Q2 Why is rubber used for tyres? Use some of the words above to help you answer.

It is used because it is...
....

....

....

Q3 Why do most metal saucepans have non-metal handles?

Non-metals are...
....

....

....

Q4 Match the following materials (on the left) to the word which best describes them.

toffee bar

electrical plug casing

compass needle

horse shoe

diamond

malleable when heated

hard

tasty

insulator

magnetic

If you're stuck... see Page 41 of our KS3 Revision Guide (Levels 3-6)

Solids, Liquids and Gases

Q1 Complete the table by writing in whether you think the substance is solid, liquid or gas.

Substance	Solid, Liquid or Gas
Cheese	
Treacle	
Steam	
Jelly	
Glass	
Petrol	
Paper	
Dry Air	

Q2 Complete the crossword by answering the clues and filling in the boxes.

Clues:

Down

1. One way of making a gas occupy a smaller volume is by .... it. (11)
4. Another way of saying how much 'space' a substance takes up. (6)

Across

2. Hardness is a useful .... of diamond (8)
3. The number of states of matter (5)
5. The hardest state of matter to squash (5)
6. This state of matter always matches the shape of its container (6)
7. The least dense of all the states of matter (3)

Solids, Liquids and Gases

Q3 For each of the diagrams below, write down whether it is solid, liquid or gas.

A

B

C

answer

answer

answer

Q4 Ice floats in water. What does this tell you about the density of ice compared to that of water? Why is this unusual?

....

....

....

Q5 Complete the following sentences using the words given in the cloud.

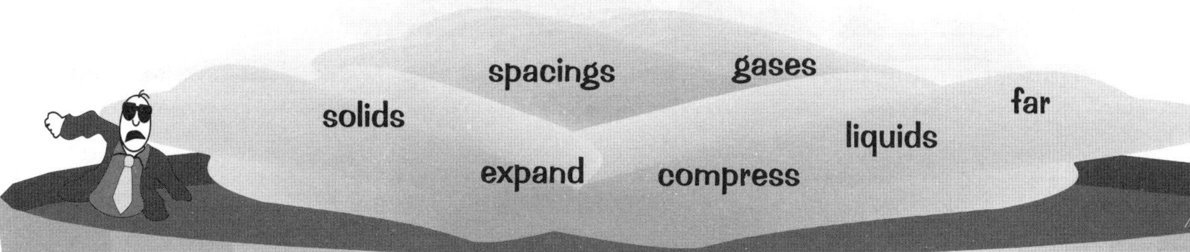

Solids, liquids and gases all have different ____________ between

their particles. The particles in a gas are quite ____________

apart compared to the particles in liquids and solids. Because of

this, it is very easy to ____________ a gas but not so easy to do

the same to a liquid or solid. ____________ will take the shape of

any container they are put in, whereas ____________ keep their

shape. Finally, ____________ will ____________ to fill any

available space in a container.

If you're stuck... see Page 42 of our KS3 Revision Guide (Levels 3-6)

Physical Changes

Q1 Look at the diagram below. What are the names given to the different changes of state? One has been done for you.

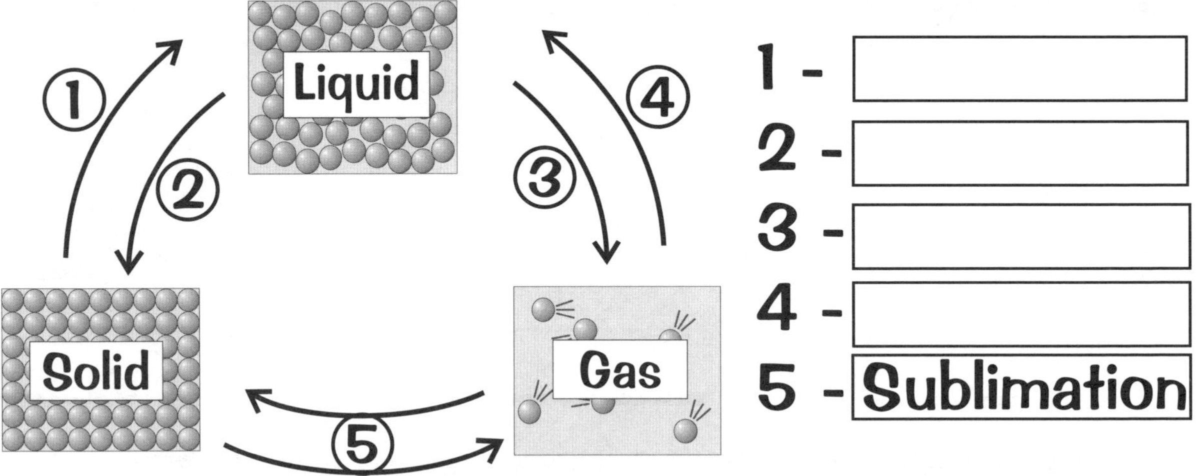

Q2 Which state must be supplied with the most energy to turn it into a gas? Explain your answer.

....

....

Q3 When energy is supplied to a solid, what happens to the particles within it? Answer in terms of the energies of the particles and the distances between them.

....

....

....

Q4 What is diffusion? Explain how a nasty smell might spread across your classroom.

....

....

....

....

....

....

....

Physical Changes

Q5 Fill in the blanks in the heating curve using the words given in the word box.

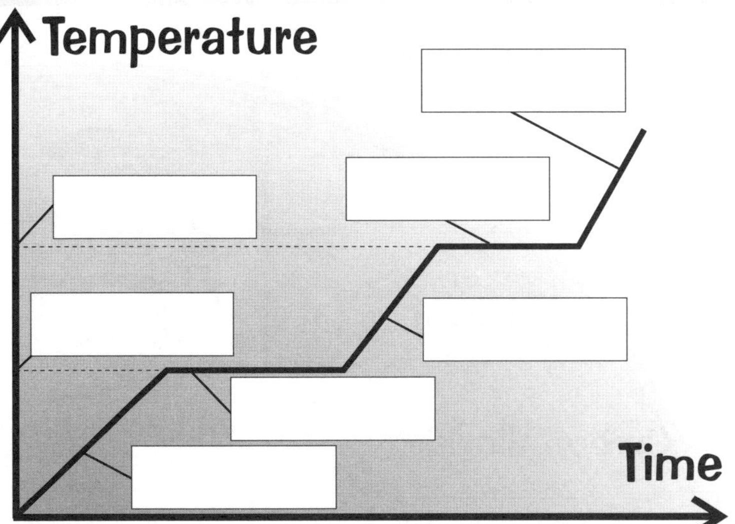

Q6 Match the correct word to its description. The first has been done for you.

The name given to the solid being dissolved — solution

The liquid that the solid is being dissolved into — saturated

The name given to the mixture of the dissolving solid and liquid — solubility

If the solid will dissolve, it is known as... — solute

But if the solid won't dissolve, it is known as... — solvent

If the liquid won't allow you to dissolve any more solid in it, it is... — soluble

The amount of solid a liquid will allow to dissolve in it — insoluble

Q7 Draw a labelled diagram in the box below to show how you would measure the freezing point of water. You should use a thermometer, filter funnel, conical flask/ beaker and ice.

Atoms and Elements

Q1 Which of the following are elements, which are compounds and which are neither? Put an **E**, a **C** or an **N** in the box next to the substance.

Carbon ☐

My pet hamster ☐

Air ☐

Uranium ☐

All Saints ☐

Helium ☐

Nitrogen ☐

Carbon dioxide ☐

Q2 The Periodic Table contains all the elements.

What is a group and a period in the Periodic Table?

....

....

....

Q3 Fill in the blanks in the following passage using the words provided.

Elements consist of one type of _________________. Elements can't be split up into anything simpler by _______________ methods. There are about _______________ different elements. Each one has a name and a shorthand _______________, e.g. Carbon, C. Everything on Earth is made up of _______________. The Periodic Table is made up of groups and periods. Some groups have names, such as group 1, the _______________ metals, group 7, the _______________ and group 0, the _______________ gases.

chemical
atom
100
halogens
elements
alkali
symbol
noble

Q4 Of the three diagrams below, which is a pure element? Tick the box.

☐   ☐   ☐

Compounds

Q1 What is the difference between an element and a compound?

....

....

....

Q2 Divide the following into two sets, *elements* and *compounds*, by writing them on the correct lines below.

Sulphur Magnesium Oxide Water Lead Carbon Dioxide Sodium Chloride Oxygen Sulphuric Acid Helium Calcium Sulphur Dioxide Carbon Monoxide Chlorine

Elements:

....

....

Compounds:

....

....

Q3 What elements do the following compounds contain?

carbon dioxide ....

copper sulphate ....

Q4 Name a compound that contains the following elements...

iron, sulphur and oxygen ....

hydrogen and sulphur ....

Properties of Metals

Q1 Shade in the part of the Periodic Table (below) that corresponds to _metals_.

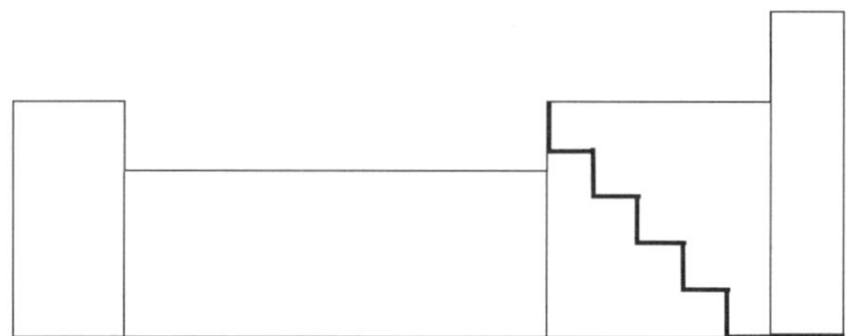

Q2 Describe some of the main differences between metals and non-metals. Use the following words and phrases in your answer.

> melting point densities boiling point
> Periodic Table good conductors of heat & electricity
> bad conductors of heat & electricity

....

....

....

Q3 Some pretty pictures describing the marvellous properties of metals are shown below. Under each picture write down what property is being demonstrated.

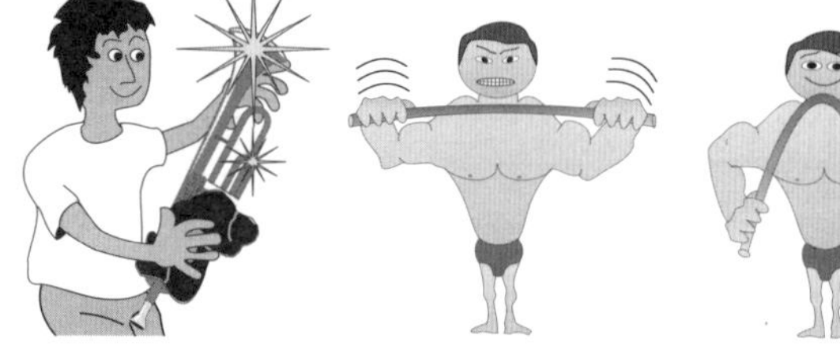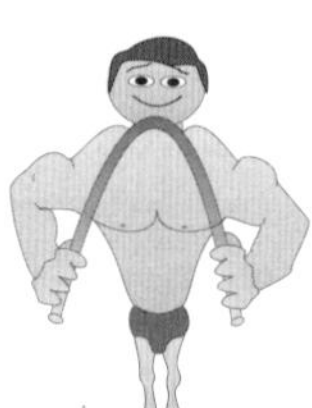

....

Q4 Match the following metals up to their common uses (think about why you would choose that use for the metal).

1. Copper	A. Used for rust prevention
2. Lead	B. Used for bridges
3. Aluminium	C. Used for wiring
4. Gold	D. Used to keep out radiation
5. Bronze	E. Used in thermometers
6. Steel	F. Used for making statues
7. Zinc	G. Used for jewellery
8. Mercury	H. Used for aircraft

Properties of Non-metals

Q1 What state are most non-metals in at room temperature? What does this tell you about the particles in non-metals? (hint — think about the 'Physical Changes' section)

....

....

....

Q2 A few diagrams of non-metals are given below. What properties of non-metals do you think they are describing? Write your answers in the boxes.

Q3 Look at the table below, then complete parts a) - d):

Element	Symbol	Melting Point (°C)	Boiling Point (°C)	State at 20°C
Sulphur		112	444	
Oxygen		-218	-183	
Bromine		-7	58	
Neon		-248	-246	
Iodine		114	183	

a) Write in the symbol of each element.

b) Write in the state of each element at room temperature (20°C).

c) Tick the non-metal which is a liquid at room temperature.

d) In which state would you find the majority of non-metals at room temperature?

....

     If you're stuck... see Page 48 of our KS3 Revision Guide (Levels 3-6) ☺

Mixtures

Q1   Tick the explanation which best describes a mixture.

- ◯ A single substance.
- ◯ A number of substances.
- ◯ Several substances combined. Separable by physical means.
- ◯ Several elements combined. Only separable by chemical means.

Q2   Four important ways of separating things are listed below.

Join up the parts of the words to show them.

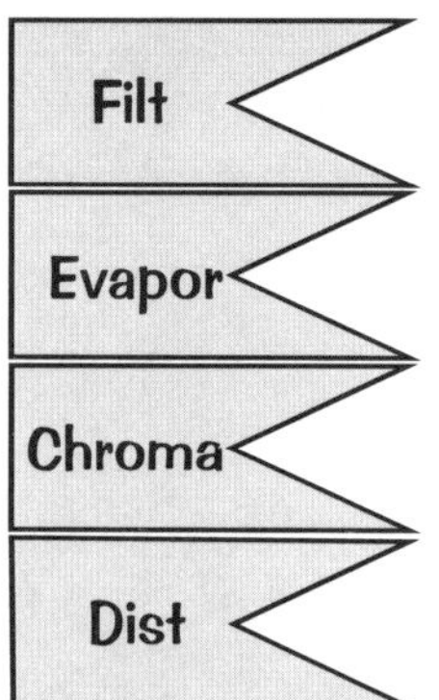

Filt — tography

Evapor — ration

Chroma — illation

Dist — ation

Q3   Byron was told that ink is a mixture of dye and water. He decided to test this theory by using the apparatus shown.

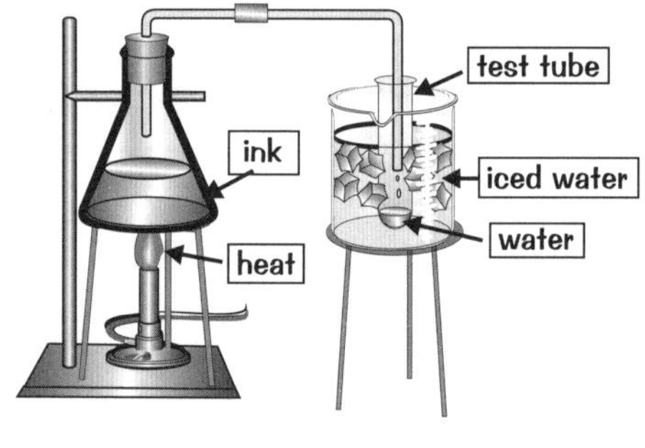

After heating for a while he found that a clear liquid was formed in the test tube.

Answer the following questions.

a)   **Why was ice used in the beaker?**

....

....

b)   **How could Byron show that this clear liquid was water?**

....

....

c) Which of these statements is true about this experiment?

◯ The dyes in the ink boil off, cool and are collected.

◯ The ink boils off, cools and is then collected.

◯ The water in the ink boils off, cools and is then collected.

◯ The steam pushes the ink out of the flask.

Q4 *Clive, a well known local scientist, discovered a dent in the door of his new red car. He suspected three clumsy neighbours, each of which had red paint on the bumpers of their green cars — one of them must have dented his pride and joy. Tearfully, he removed samples of red paint form each neighbours bumper and examined the colours using chromatography.*

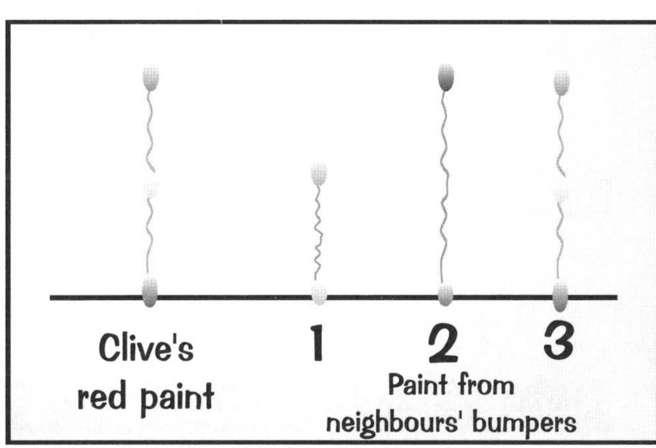

a) How many paint pigments are found in the red paint of Clive's car?

....

....

b) What must be used to make the paints split up into the various pigments?

....

c) Explain in detail how chromatography is being used in this investigation.

....

....

....

d) Which neighbour appears to be the clumsy one who bumped Clive's car?

....

Geological Changes

The rock cycle involves changing the three rock types (*igneous, sedimentary and metamorphic*) from one to another. The picture below illustrates the rock cycle.

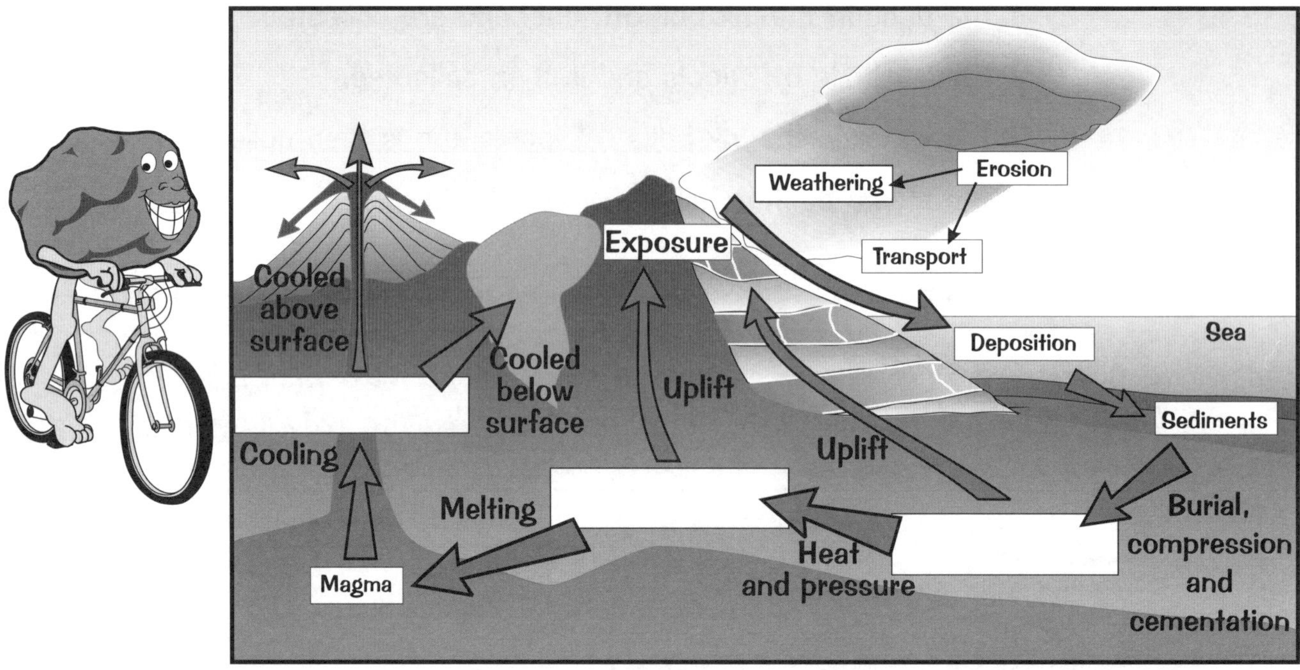

Q1 Complete the rock cycle picture by putting in the three rock types listed below:

igneous rocks

sedimentary rocks

metamorphic rocks

Q2 Complete the following paragraphs by filling in the missing words from the list:

igneous	metamorphic	weathering	buried	compressed heat
melt	magma	sea	magma	cools rock cycle

Over millions of years rocks change from one type to another. This is called the

_________ __________ . *Rocks are broken up by* _________ *and*

washed into the _________ . *Over millions of years these become buried,*

_________ *and cemented and form sedimentary rocks.*

Sometimes these rocks become _________ *deeper into the Earth, and are*

changed by _________ *and pressure into* _________ *rocks.*

If metamorphic rocks are buried still further they can _________ *and become*

_________ . *Pressure forces the* _________ *upwards where it*

_________ *to make* _________ *rocks.*

Geological Changes

Q3   **Complete the sentences about rock types.**

Igneous rocks form from ....
....

Sedimentary rocks form from ....
....

Metamorphic rocks form from ....
....

Q4   **Look at the descriptions of various rocks below. Try to identify each type of rock as Igneous, Sedimentary or Metamorphic then tick the correct column in the box below.**

Basalt

Chalk

Slate

Grit

Granite

Marble

Obsidian

Sandstone

Marl

Quartzite

A dark rock with small crystals, formed on the surface of the Earth.

A white rock formed from the shells of sea animals which collected at the bottom of shallow seas.

A dark rock showing crystals and layers. It was formed by shale being changed by heat and pressure.

Rock formed from small particles stuck together.

A speckled rock. The speckles are different crystals that have formed from melted rock which cooled slowly inside the earth.

A usually white, hard rock. It is made from crystals, but also shows layers. It is formed from chalk or limestone by heat and pressure.

A glassy rock formed by volcanoes. The melted rock has cooled very quickly, so crystals are unable to form.

A rock formed from small grains of sand which have been squeezed tightly together.

A rock made from small, dark grey fragments which have been squeezed together.

A crystalline rock which has been formed by changes due to heat and pressure within the earth.

Rock	Igneous	Sedimentary	Metamorphic
Basalt			
Chalk			
Slate			
Grit			
Granite			
Marble			
Obsidian			
Sandstone			
Marl			
Quartzite			

If you're stuck... see Page 58/59 of our KS3 Revision Guide (Levels 3-6)

Useful Chemical Change

Q1 **The statements below are about chemical reactions. Tick the circle.**

		True as a true thing	False as a false thing	Don't rightly know
a)	Mass isn't lost when the reactants turn into the products.	◯	◯	◯
b)	A word equation doesn't show what's going on in a reaction.	◯	◯	◯
c)	Chemical reactions involve temporary changes.	◯	◯	◯
d)	Reactions always involve a change in energy.	◯	◯	◯
e)	Energy is either given out or taken in.	◯	◯	◯
f)	The temperature in a reaction will only go up.	◯	◯	◯
g)	Visible changes never occur in the reaction mixture.	◯	◯	◯

Q2 **Five very useful, chemical reactions are listed below. For each say why they are so useful.**

a) Combustion is useful because ....

....

b) Fermentation is useful because ....

....

c) Smelting is useful because ....

....

d) Neutralisation is useful because ....

....

e) Electrolysis is useful because ....

....

Less Useful Chemical Change

Q3 Felicity was investigating what makes things rust. She decided to set up the apparatus as shown below.

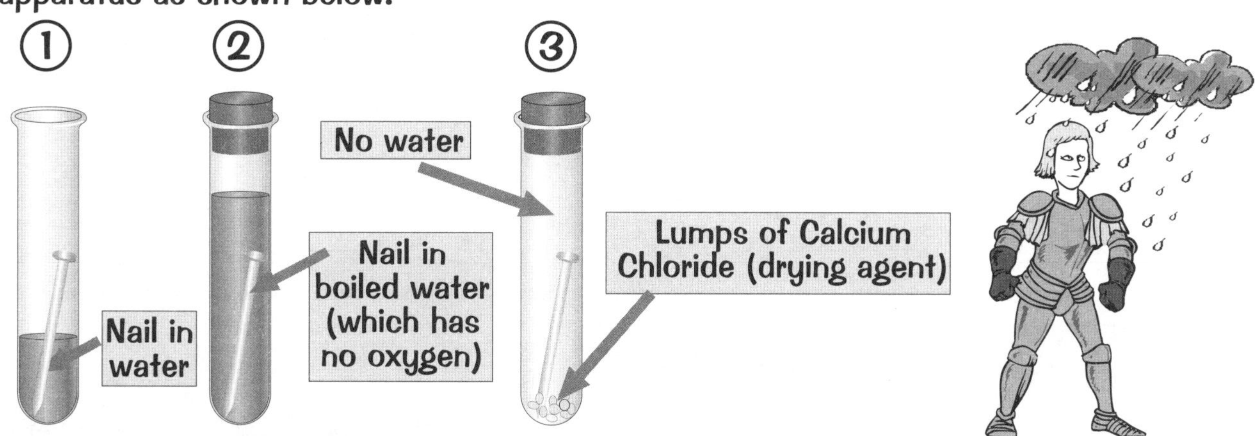

a) Complete the table below with the results you would expect her to get.

Tube	Colour of nail before	Colour of nail after
1		
2		
3		

b) In which tube(s) does rusting occur?

....

c) Why is calcium chloride used in this investigation?

....

d) What two things must be in contact with iron for it to rust?

....

Q4 The pictures below show how you can stop rusting. Briefly say how each method stops the reaction of rusting.

....

....

If you're stuck... see Page 62/63 of our KS3 Revision Guide (Levels 3-6) ☺

Reactions of Metals

Q1   Study the information below and then answer the questions.

> iron reacts slowly with water
>
> potassium is hard to remove from its ore
>
> potassium reacts violently with water
>
> copper doesn't react with water
>
> copper is easy to remove from its ore
>
> iron is removed from its ore using carbon

a)   **Put the metals in order of reactivity.**

1) ....

2) ....

3) ....

b)   **Which metal would you choose to make a water pipe from? Explain your answer.**

Metal ....

Reason ....

....

c)   These three metals were then put in three test tubes of hydrochloric acid. The results were mistakenly written on a bit of scrap paper, and so are all jumbled up.

Sort out the results into the nice table below.

Reaction in acid	Potassium	Copper	Iron
Observations			

Displacement Reactions

Q1 A piece of an unknown metal **X** was placed into a solution of three salts, copper sulphate, magnesium sulphate and iron sulphate. The results of this are shown below.

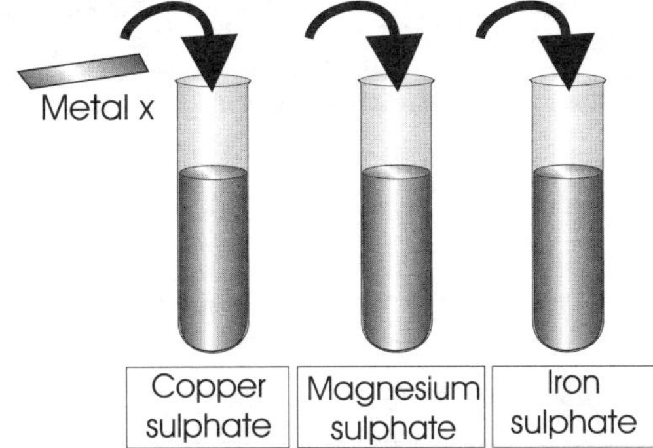

Results

Salt solution	Copper sulphate	Magnesium sulphate	Iron sulphate
Result with X added	Orange solid appeared on metal	No reaction	Grey solid appeared on metal

a) Did a reaction happen between metal **X** and copper sulphate?

....

b) Is metal **X** more or less reactive than copper?

....

c) Did a reaction happen between metal **X** and magnesium sulphate?

....

d) Is metal **X** more or less reactive than magnesium?

....

e) Did a reaction happen between metal **X** and iron sulphate?

....

f) Is metal **X** more or less reactive than iron?

....

g) What is the name given to a reaction where one metal takes the place of another?

....

h) Put copper, magnesium, iron and metal **X** in order of reactivity. *(most reactive to least reactive).*

....

Acids and Alkalis

Q1 Place a tick in the box next to each of the following statements to indicate which is True and which is False.

	True	False
All acids are dangerous	☐	☐
All alkalis are dangerous	☐	☐
All acids are dissolved in water	☐	☐
All alkalis are dissolved in water	☐	☐
Acids can burn skin	☐	☐
Alkalis feel soapy	☐	☐
Lemons contain alkali	☐	☐
Acids taste sweet	☐	☐
Acids stop indigestion	☐	☐
All acids are corrosive	☐	☐
Acids have a pH above 7	☐	☐
Acids have a pH below 7	☐	☐
The pH scale goes from 0 to 14	☐	☐

Q2 Name three common acids you might find in the lab.

1) ....

2) ....

3) ....

Q3 Name three common alkalis you might find in the lab.

1) ....

2) ....

3) ....

Acids and Alkalis

Q4 Circle the hazchem symbol that should be used on a bottle of bench acid.

Q5 Circle the hazchem symbol that should be used on a bottle of bench alkali.

Q6 List three things you should always do when using acids or alkalis in the laboratory.

1) ....

2) ....

3) ....

Q7 Tick which of the following contain acids.

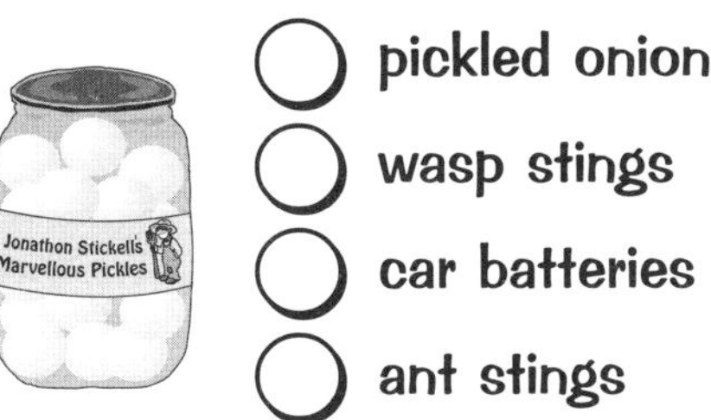

- ◯ pickled onions
- ◯ wasp stings
- ◯ car batteries
- ◯ ant stings

Q8 Which of the following contain alkalis?

- ◯ oven cleaner
- ◯ soaps
- ◯ fertilisers
- ◯ lime

Q9 Acids react with metals like zinc to make hydrogen gas and react with rocks like limestone to produce carbon dioxide.

What are the tests for hydrogen and carbon dioxide?

....

....

....

If you're stuck... see Page 71/72 of our KS3 Revision Guide (Levels 3-6) ☺

The pH Scale and Indicators

Q1   Litmus is an indicator. In acids it goes red and in alkali it goes blue.

What is an indicator?

....

....

Q2   **Colour in the pH chart below with the correct colours for Universal Indicator solution.**

pH   1   2   3   4   5   6   7   8   9   10   11   12   13   14

_ _ _ ACIDS _ _ _ _ _ | _ _ _ ALKALIS _ _ _

NEUTRAL

Q3   **What values of pH would you expect for:**

a)   Lemon juice ....

b)   Oven cleaner ....

c)   Lime (calcium hydroxide) ....

d)   Sodium Chloride (common salt) ....

e)   Hydrochloric acid ....

Q4   Look at the following information:

Magnesium oxide pH 10

Ethanoic acid pH 3-4

Potassium chloride pH 7

Potassium hydroxide pH 13

Hydrogen chloride pH 2

Choose an example which is...

a)   A strong acid ....

b)   A weak acid ....

c)   A weak alkali ....

d)   A neutral substance ....

e)   A strong alkali ....

Neutralisation — A Useful Acid Reaction

Q1 Your stomach contains about a litre of acid which helps digest food. Occasionally some acid finds its way out of your stomach — this is called indigestion. It can be quite painful, but neutralisation can be used to cancel out the acid pain.

a) Name a chemical substance which could be used to reduce the acid in your stomach.

....

b) What is produced when the acid is neutralised?

....

c) "Antacid" is the name given to the medicines which neutralise acids in the stomach.

Why are they called "antacids"?

....

d) The general equation for these reactions has been started below.
Complete the equation by writing in the products.

Acid　　+　　Alkali　　→　　........................　+　　........................

Q2a) Complete the table below which show the pH range that some plants prefer.

b) What may cause the soil to get too acidic?

....

....

....

Plant	Soil pH which the plant likes
Potato	
Broccoli	
Carrot	
Onion	

c) What will happen to a plant if the pH is wrong?

....

d) "Lime" is used to neutralise acidic soil — what chemical substance is "lime"?

....

Less Useful Acid Reactions

Q1 What is the natural pH of rain-water?

....

Q2 Pollutants in the air make rain-water more acidic.

Will the pH of the rain-water go up or go down with pollutants in it?

....

Q3 Give the name of two pollutants found in air which make rain-water more acidic.

....

Q4 Look at the two limestone statues below. One has been affected by acid rain, the other hasn't. Explain in as much detail as possible how and why each statue looks different.

....

....

....

....

....

....

....

....

....

....

Q5 Stephen put an old tooth into a glass of cola. The next day he found that the tooth had turned soft and the surface of the tooth had been removed. He tested the pH of the drink and found that it was acidic.

What advice would you give to someone who drinks lots of cola everyday?

....

....

Static Charge

Q1 How would you use a duster to charge a plastic rod?

....

....

Q2 There are two types of charge; positive and negative.

Which type moves when an object is being charged up?

....

Q3 Electric charge can produce forces that pull things together (attract) or push them apart (repel). We call these forces electrostatic forces.

Complete the following table by writing whether the force between the two charges will "attract" or "repel" them.

Charge 1	Charge 2	Force between
positive	positive	
positive	negative	
negative	positive	
negative	negative	

Q4 The gold leaf electroscope is a piece of equipment used to study static electric charge. The diagram shows a gold leaf electroscope that has no overall charge.

a) When there is no overall charge on the gold leaf electroscope, will the leaves be open or closed?

....

b) If some positive charge is brought up close to the top plate, will the leaves open or close?

....

c) Suppose the top plate was charged so that the leaves were separated. How could you make the leaves move back together again?

....

....

If you're stuck... see Page 74 of our KS3 Revision Guide (Levels 3-6) ☺

Electricity and Current

Q1 What do we call a material that will carry an electric current?

....

Q2 What do we call a material that won't carry an electric current?

....

Q3 Put a tick by the materials below that will carry a current.

Q4 Circle the correct words to complete the following sentences.

Electric current is a flow of _charge_ / _water_. It flows from _negative_ / _positive_ to _negative_ / _positive_. Conventional current flows from _negative_ / _positive_ to _negative_ / _positive_.

For current to flow, a _power source_ / _bulb_ and a _bulb_ / _complete circuit_ are needed. The current flowing out of a battery is _the same as_ / _more than_ the current flowing back into it.

Q5 Look at the circuits below. Put a tick in the boxes by the bulbs that will light up.

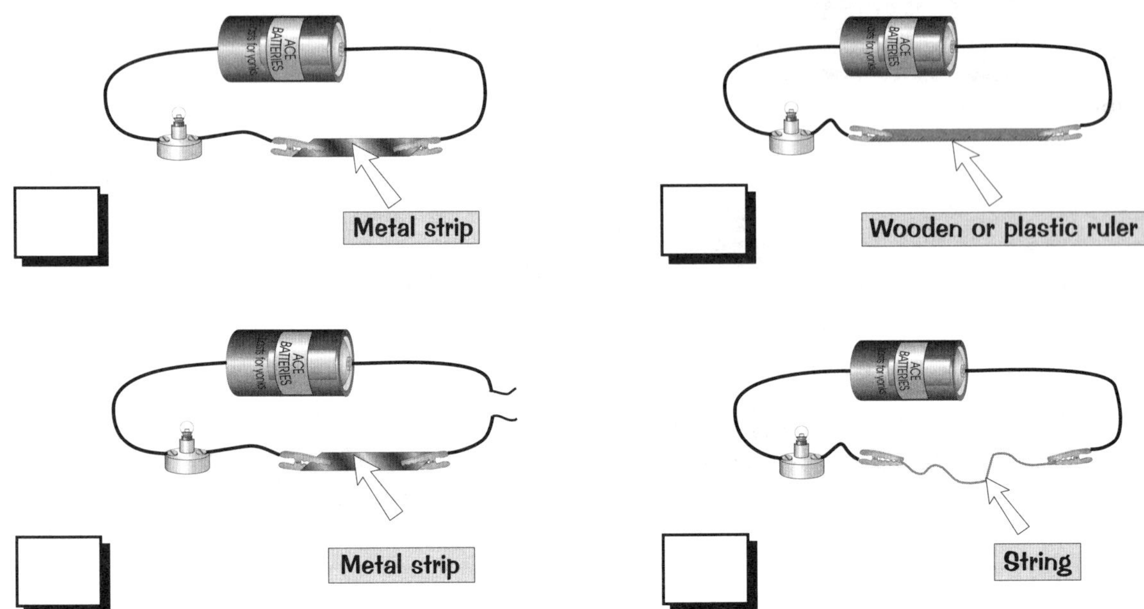

Electric Current in Circuits

Q1 Draw the symbols for the following devices. One is done for you.

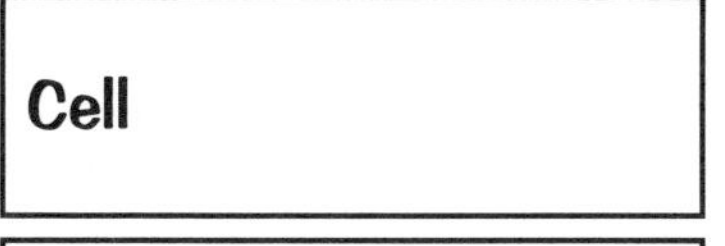

Cell	Ammeter	Bulb
Switch	Battery	Motor ———(M)———

Q2 An electric motor converts electrical energy to what type of energy?

....

Q3 Study the following circuit diagrams and answer the questions below. All the lamps have the same resistance.

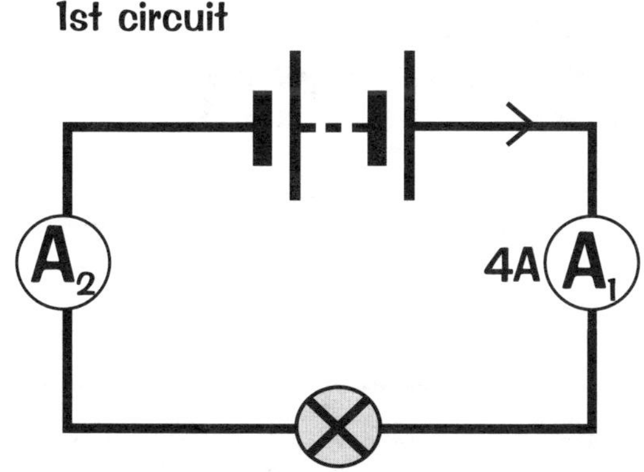

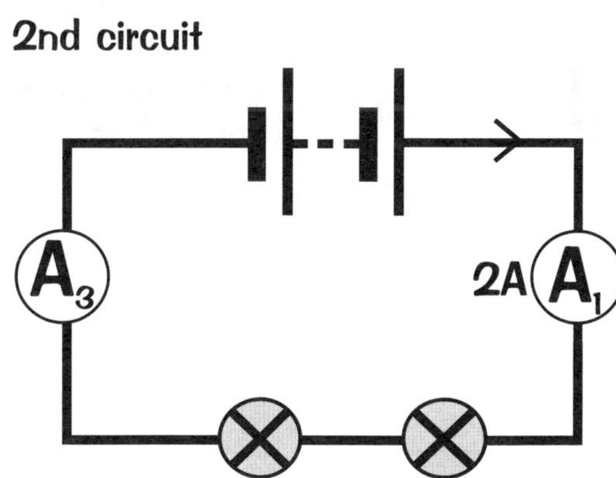

a) What is the value of the current flowing through A₂?

....

b) What is the value of the current flowing through A₃?

....

c) Is the total resistance greater in the first circuit or the second?

....

Q4 What is meant by the term "short circuit"?

....

....

....

If you're stuck... see Page 76 of our KS3 Revision Guide (Levels 3-6) ☺

Magnets and Electromagnets

Q1 Name three magnetic elements.

1) .... 2) .... 3) ....

Q2 Draw the magnetic field lines for the magnet shown below.

| N   S |

Q3 Beneath are shown two pairs of magnets without the poles labelled. One pair are attracting each other and the other pair are repelling each other.

Label the poles of the magnets "N" or "S" and draw the field lines.

Attracting   *Repelling*

Q4 Draw a diagram to show how you would make an electromagnet.

(You may use a *battery*, *wire* and an *iron cylinder*).

Force and Movement

Q1 Circle the right formula used for calculating speed.

$$\text{Speed} = \frac{\text{Time}}{\text{Distance}} \qquad \text{Speed} = \frac{\text{Distance}}{\text{Time}}$$

$$\text{Speed} = \text{Time} \times \text{Distance}$$

Q2 List the five things my toy car might do if it was acted on by an unbalanced force.

1) ....

2) ....

3) ....

4) ....

5) ....

Q3 Circle the correct words to complete the following sentences.

Forces are measured in *kilograms* / *newtons*. An unbalanced force is needed to *keep something* / *start something* moving. If all forces are balanced a moving object will *slow down* / *keep going*. Weight is a type of *force* / *mass* and is measured in *newtons* / *kilograms*.

Q4 Spot is a stupid dog. Whenever he goes out for a walk with his owner, Lynda, he always starts pulling on his lead and tries to run off.

a) Mark on the diagram which way Spot pulls and which way Lynda pulls.

b) What will happen to Lynda and Spot if the lead breaks?

....

....

Air Resistance and Friction

Q1   Use arrows to mark on the truck the following forces.
(It is going forwards).

> Driving force,   Friction,
> Weight,   Reaction of road.

a)   If the car's engine failed at 70 mph on the motorway which force would vanish?

....

b)   What would friction do to the speed of the car after the engine failed?

....

Q2   The pictures below show the fall of a parachutist from an aeroplane.

a)   For each part of the skydive draw pairs of arrows to show how the vertical forces
act on the parachutist.   Use big arrows to represent big forces.

Getting faster

Steady speed

Getting slower

Steady speed

Stopped

b)   Which is greater, the drag force when free falling at steady speed or the drag force
with the parachute open at steady speed?

....

Force and Rotation

Q1   Machines are things that make tasks easier. Machines can be very simple. The prize for the simplest goes to the ramp but a close runner-up is the lever.

Which person will find it easiest to lift their rock? Circle your choice.

Q2   Circle the correct words to complete the following sentences.

When you are using a lever, the longer the lever on your side of the pivot the _greater_ / _smaller_ the turning force about the pivot. Using a long lever with the pivot close to the load makes lifting a large load _harder_ / _easier_. Using a long lever with the pivot close to the load makes the distance moved by the load _small_ / _large_.

Q3   Mark on each of the following diagrams the loads, efforts and pivots.

An example has been done for you.

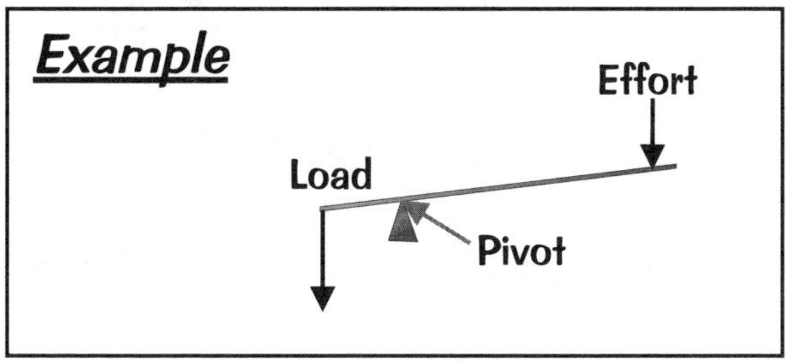

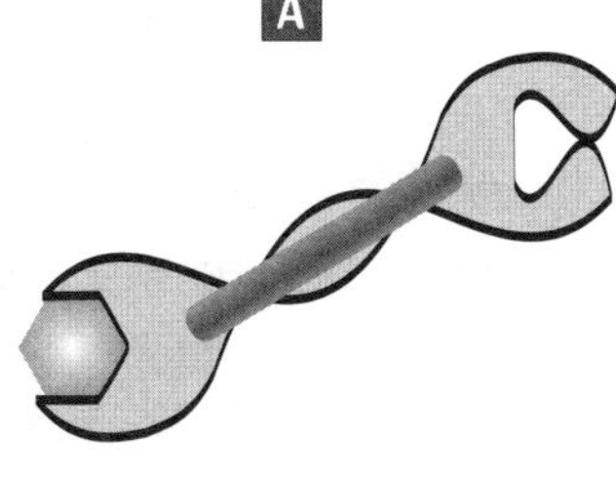

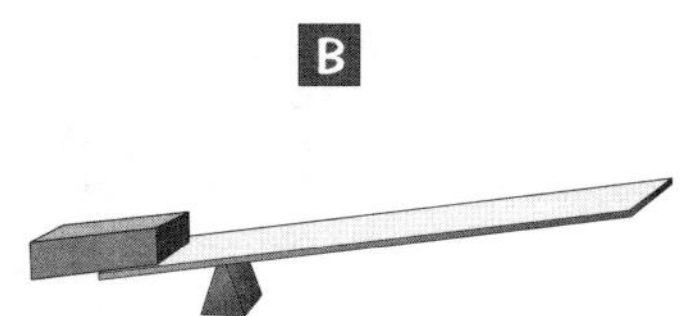

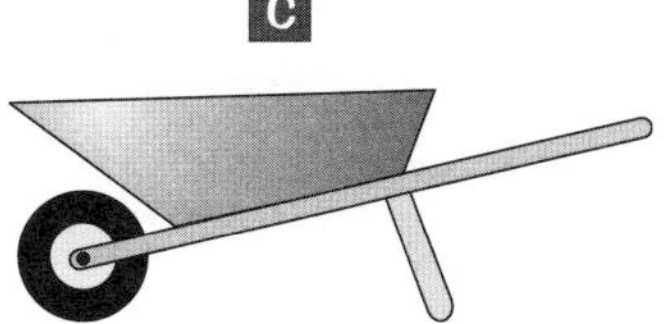

   If you're stuck... see Page 84 of our KS3 Revision Guide (Levels 3-6) ☺

Pressure

Q1 In modern tank guns the projectile (bullet) is held in a wide bottomed cup called a sabot, inside the barrel. When the projectile leaves the barrel the sabot breaks away as the projectile heads towards the target.

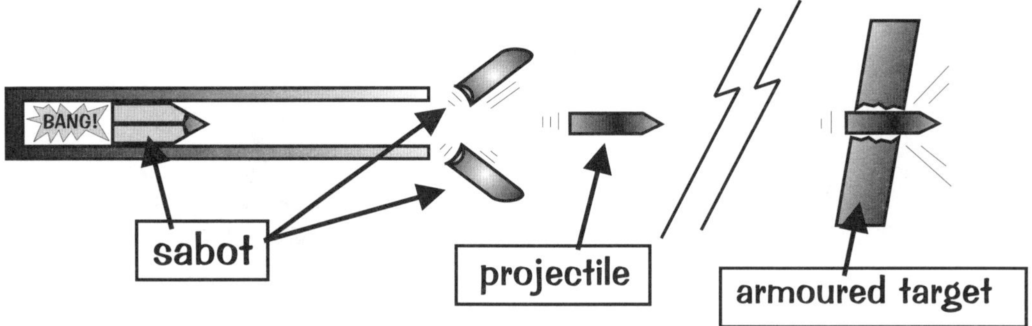

a) If there is a maximum pressure that the gun barrel can stand then changing the area of the bottom of the sabot will alter the force on the projectile.

> If the area of the bottom of the sabot is increased, will the force acting on it from the bang increase or decrease?

....

b) > What effect will this have on the speed of the bullet as it leaves the barrel?

....

c) > If the bullet is to penetrate a target, is it better for the bullet to be narrow or thick? Why?

....

....

Q2 Big Foot and his mate Little Foot had a race across the Himalayas. Big Foot weighs more than Little Foot but to the surprise of them both, Little Foot got stuck in the snow.

> Explain in terms of pressure why it was Little Foot who got stuck and not Big Foot.

....

....

....

....

Properties of Light

Q1 Circle the correct word in the brackets to complete the sentence.

"Light always travels in (curved / straight) lines."

Q2 In the picture a torch is shining light on to a man and casting a shadow.

Put the following labels in the white boxes.

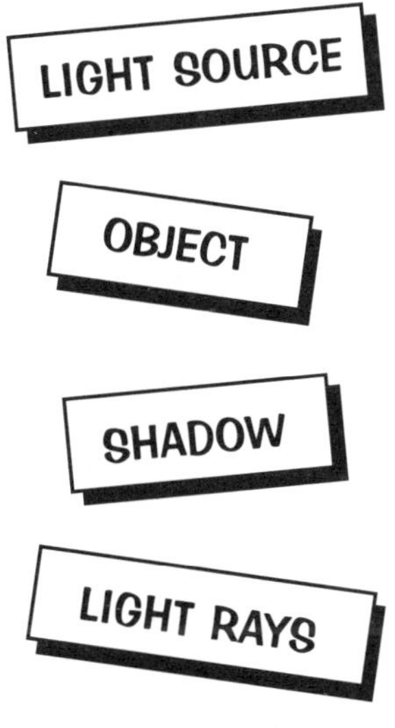

Q3 Explain how shadows are formed.

....

....

....

Q4 We see non-luminous objects because light reflects off them and enters our eyes.

Look at the picture below and show the path of a ray of light from the light source so Pedro can see the bird.

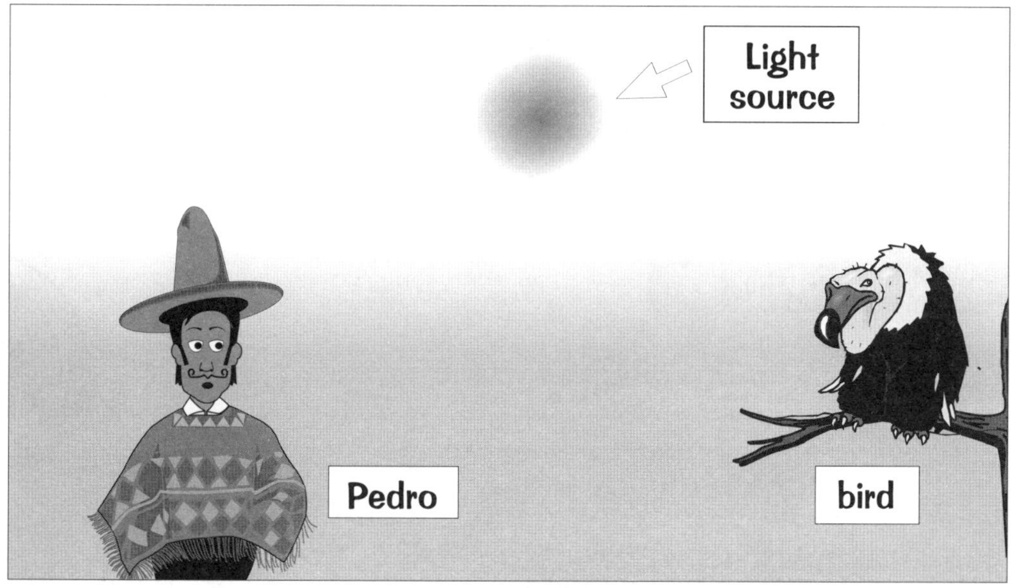

If you're stuck... see Page 88 of our KS3 Revision Guide (Levels 3-6)

Reflection

Q1   The diagram shows light rays about to be reflected from a smooth surface.

a)   Complete the diagram to show how the light rays are reflected from this surface.

b)   Name a type of reflector with a smooth surface.

....

Q2   The diagram shows light rays about to be reflected from a rough surface.

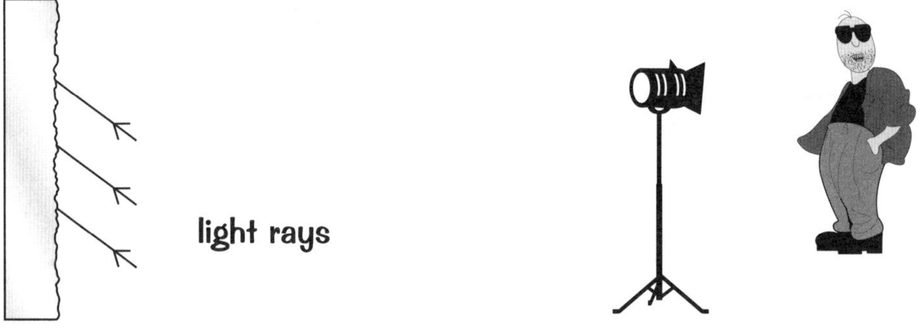

a)   Complete the diagram to show how the light rays are reflected from this surface.

b)   Most reflectors have rough surfaces.

Give two examples of a reflector with a rough surface.

....

c)   What type of reflection would you get from a piece of sandpaper?

....

Q3   List three uses of mirrors.

1) ....

2) ....

3) ....

Refraction

Q1   In physics, what is a medium?

....

Q2   When light enters glass from air it changes direction.
What is this change of direction called?

....

Q3   Glass is denser than air so light will refract when it enters and leaves a glass block.
The diagrams show rays of light in air entering a glass block.   For each one complete the path of the ray of light into and out of the block.

a)

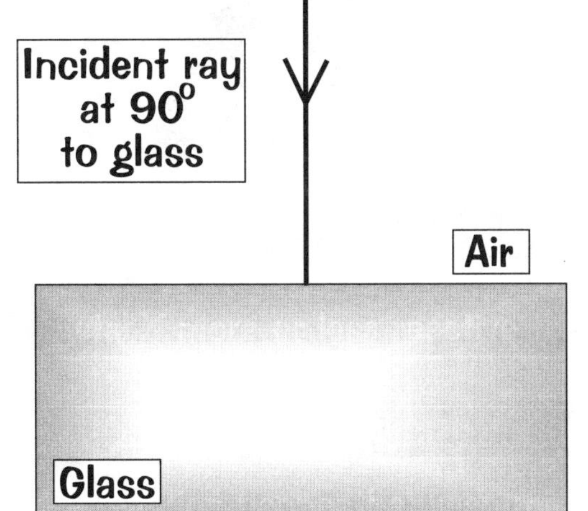

b)

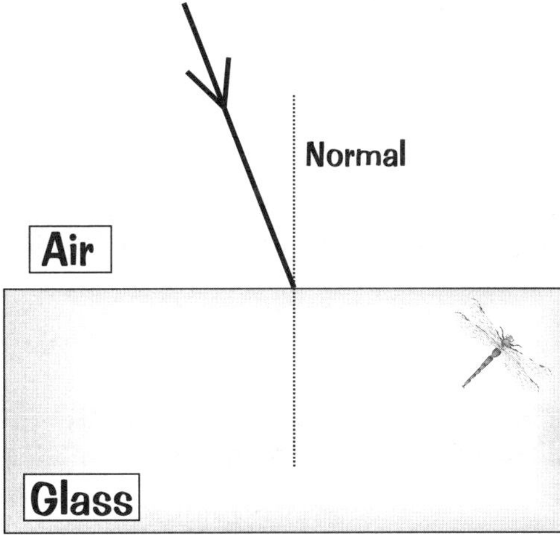

Q4   Circle the correct words in the brackets to complete the following sentences.

a) When a light ray travels from one medium into another, more dense, medium, it bends (away from / towards) the normal.

b) When a light ray travels from one medium into another, less dense, medium, it bends (away from / towards) the normal.

Colour

Q1 When white light passes through a prism it is split up into different colours.

a)

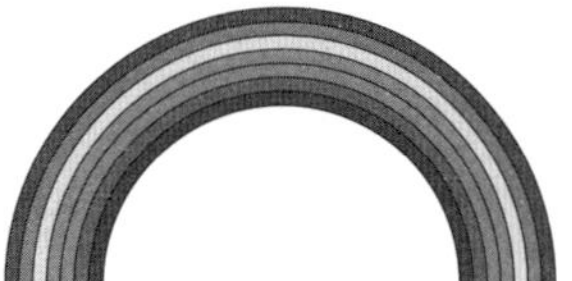

....

b) The picture shows white light passing through a prism and landing on a white screen.

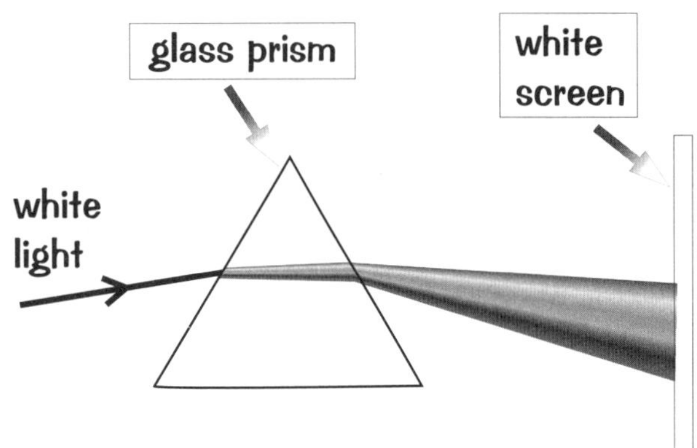

....

c)

magenta ☐	pink ☐	gold ☐	black ☐
yellow ☐	red ☐	cyan ☐	green ☐
indigo ☐	blue ☐	violet ☐	orange ☐

Q2 The diagram shows white light being passed through a coloured filter.

a)

....

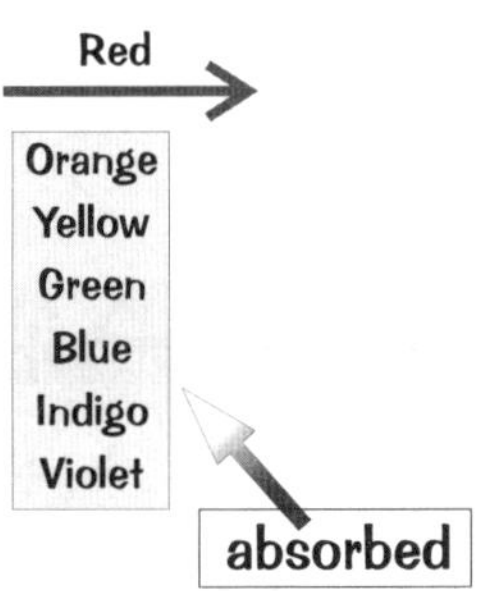

b)

....

....

Sound

Q1 The picture shows a demonstration of sound travel using a bell jar.

a) Complete the sentences by circling the correct words in brackets.

"When air is sucked out of the jar the ringing of the alarm clock inside the jar gets (louder / quieter). When all the air is removed the bell (can not be heard / stops)."

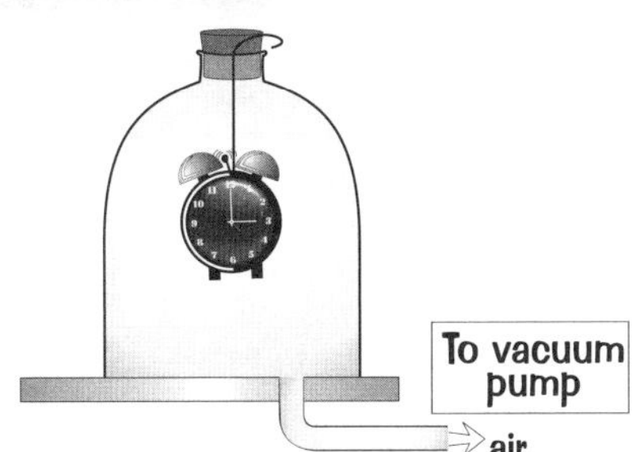

b) The ring of the alarm clock goes quiet because: (tick the correct box)

there is no air in the jar to carry the vibrations ☐

sound can not travel through the glass of the bell jar ☐

the vacuum stops the bell moving ☐

Q2 Sound waves have many properties in common with light waves. — e.g. sound diffracts _and_ light diffracts.

Give two other physical properties that sound and light have in common.

1) ....

2) ....

Q3 Sound waves can be displayed on an oscilloscope screen like the one below.

a) Which of the lines in the picture indicate the amplitude of the wave?

....

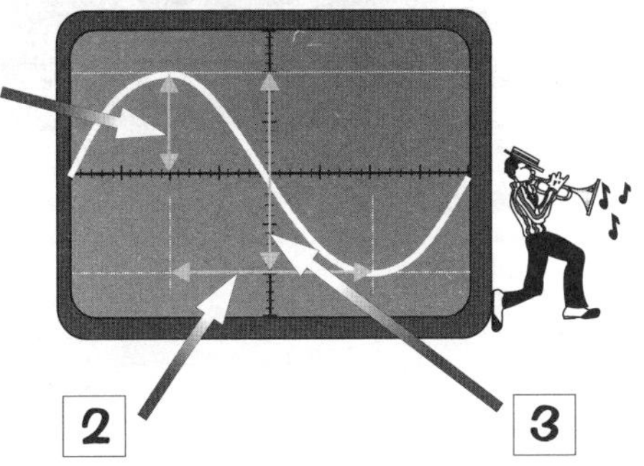

b) A wave with the same frequency but carrying more energy than the first one is fed into the oscilloscope.

i) Draw how the wave will look on the screen opposite.

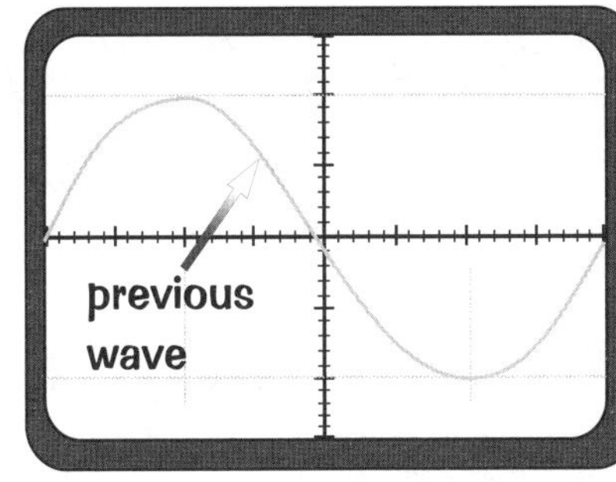

ii) What difference would you hear?

....

Hearing

Q1 The picture below shows how sound from a twanged ruler travels to the brain.

Use the following words to complete the labelling in the diagram.

particles   ruler   bones   drum   hairs   brain   cochlea

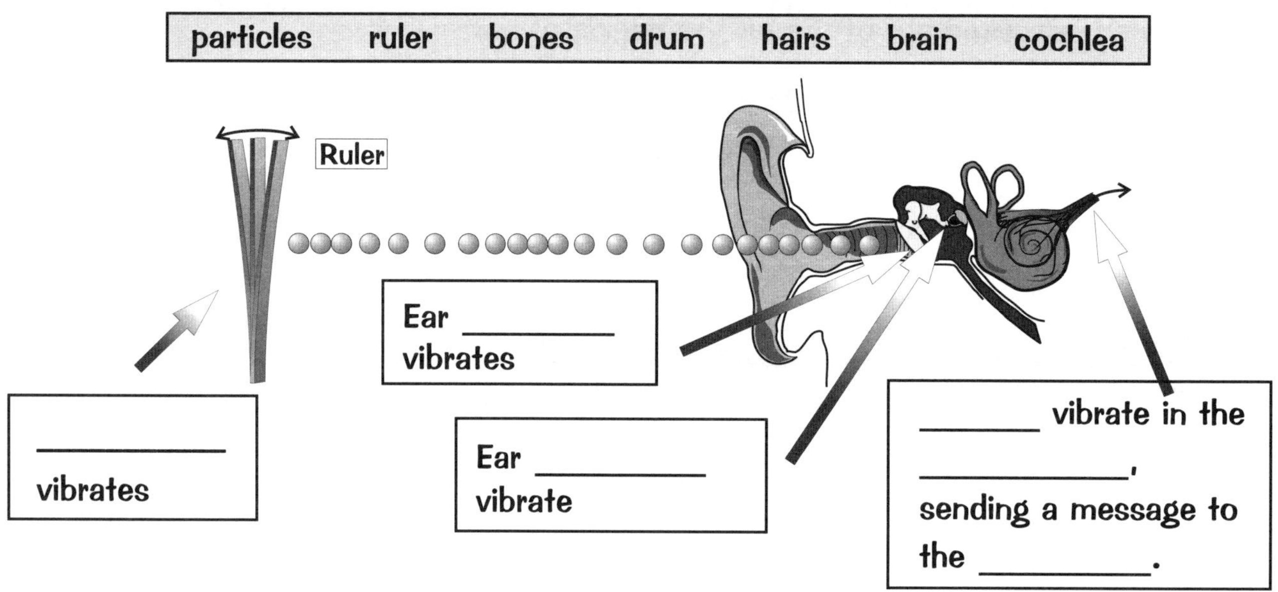

Q2 The bar chart shows the range of frequencies that people and animals can hear.

a) **Who has the most limited range of hearing?**

....

b) **Suggest a reason why dolphins need to hear such high frequency sounds.**

....

....

....

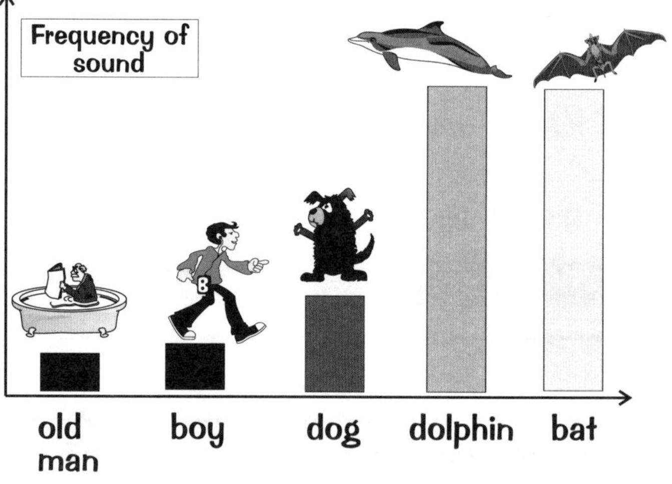

c) **Tick the correct box below to complete the following.**

"Dolphins can hear higher frequency sounds than dogs. This means that dolphins can hear sounds of a .... "

lower pitch ☐   higher pitch ☐

The Moon and Satellites

Q1 **What is a satellite?**

....

Q2 **Which of the following are satellites? Tick the correct boxes.**

The Moon ☐   The Sun ☐   The Earth ☐   The Hubble Space Telescope ☐

Q3 **Give two uses of an artificial satellite orbiting the Earth.**

1) ....

2) ....

Q4 **What is the name of the force that keeps the Moon in orbit around the Earth?**

....

Q5 The picture shows the Earth and the Moon in space.

Use two arrows to show the force of the Earth's pull on the Moon and the force of the Moon's pull on the Earth.

Q6 **Fill the gaps in the following sentences. Use the words in the "nebula". Words may be used once, more than once or not at all.**

moon 28 38 Sun colour shape refracting reflecting different same light dark

The ______________ orbits the Earth in ___________ days.

The Moon appears to change _______________ as it goes through a full orbit of

the Earth. This is because we only see the part of the Moon which is

_________________ light from the Sun. We see _________________ amounts of

the Moon's sunny side as it orbits the Earth — that's why it seems to change shape

because you can't see the _________________ bits.

Day and Night

Q1   The picture shows the Earth.

Earth

a)   Complete the labelling for "night-time" and "daytime".

b)   Draw the Earth's rotational axis on the picture.

c)   How long does it take for the Earth to rotate once on its axis? (Give your answer in hours).

....

Q2   Explain why we experience daytime and night-time on Earth.

....

....

....

Q3   Reginald lives in Scotland. He sees the Sun moving across the sky during the day.

a)   Where does the Sun rise in the morning? Tick the correct box.

in the North ☐   in the South ☐

in the West ☐   in the East ☐

b)   He sees the Sun reaching its highest point in the sky, then it begins to descend.

At what time does it begin to descend?

....

The Four Seasons

Q1 The picture below shows the Earth in four positions in its orbit around the Sun.

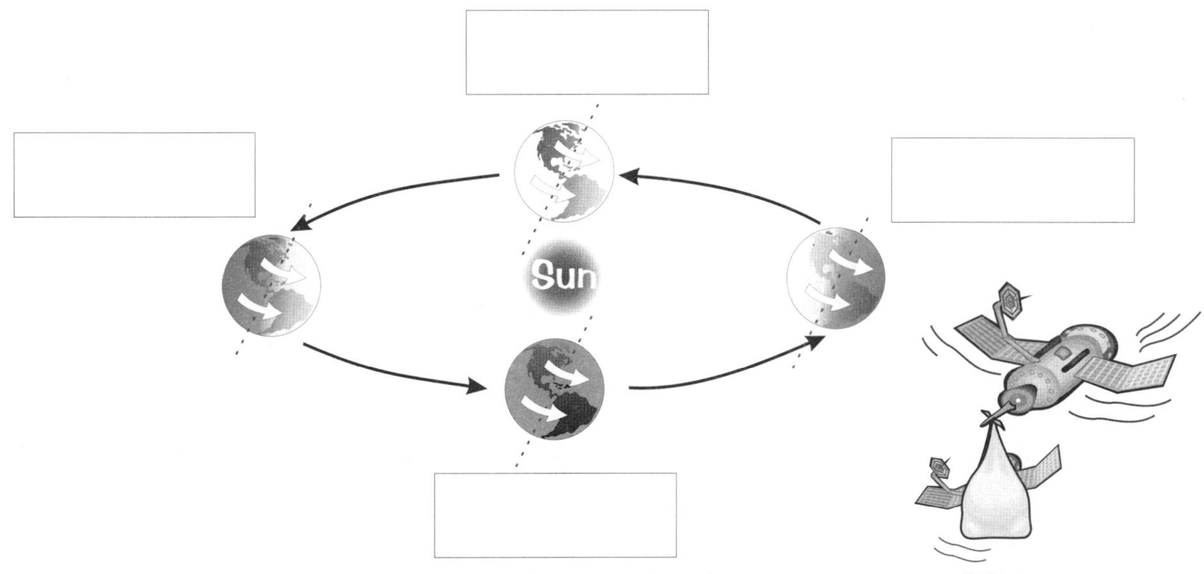

a) Label the four seasons on the diagram, for the Northern Hemisphere.

b) Shadows cast at midday are shortest during one of the seasons.

i) Which season is this?

....

ii) Explain why shadows are *generally* shortest in this season.

....

....

Q2 The Earth's axis is tilted and this is why we have seasons.
However, if there was no tilt, the countries near the equator would still have
a warmer climate than countries further north or south.

Use the picture below to help explain why this would be the case.

....

....

....

....

....

....

....

The Solar System

Q1   Is Earth a planet or a star?

....

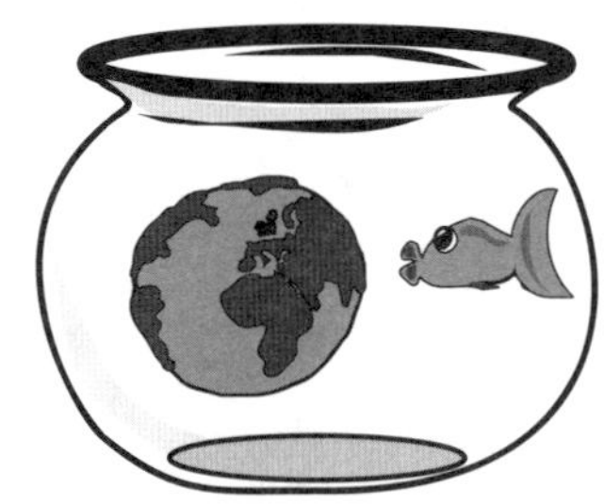

Q2   Is the Sun a planet or a star?

....

Q3   What is the main difference between a star and a planet?

....

....

Q4   The eight planets of our solar system are shown in the picture below.

Write in the names of the planets in the spaces provided.

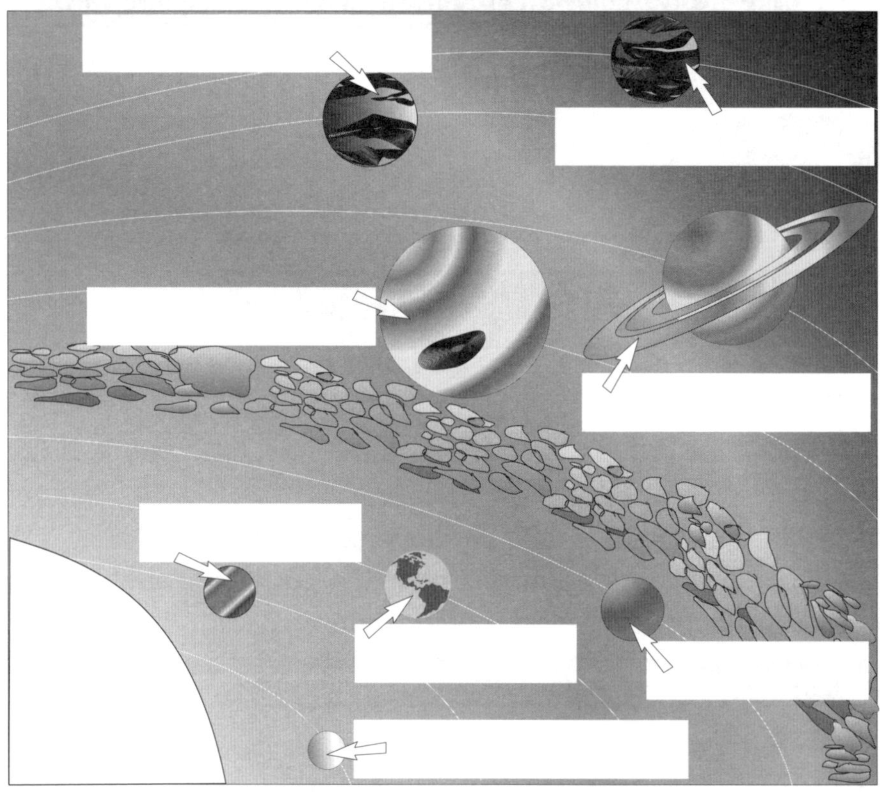

Q5   All the planets move around the Sun which lies at the centre of the Solar System.

What is the name given to the path followed by a planet going around the Sun?

....

Q6   What is the name given to the shape of a planet's path around the Sun?

....

The Solar System

Q7   What is the name of the force that keeps planets in orbit about the Sun?

....

Q8   Look at the table of data below. It shows information about the planets.

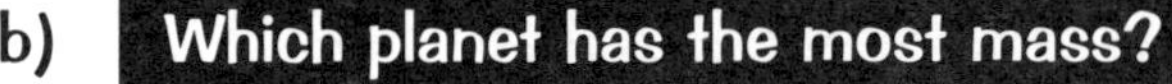

	PLANET	RELATIVE SIZE	RELATIVE MASS	MEAN DIST. FROM SUN	ORBIT TIME
INNER PLANETS	MERCURY	0.4	0.05	58	88d
	VENUS	0.9	0.8 (Earth	108 (millions	225d
	EARTH	1.0	1.0 masses)	150 of km)	365d
	MARS	0.5	0.1	228	687d
OUTER PLANETS	JUPITER	11.0	318.0	778	12y
	SATURN	9.4	95.0	1430	29y
	URANUS	4.0	15.0	2870	84y
	NEPTUNE	3.8	17.0	4500	165y

d = Earth days

y = Earth years

a)   Which planet is nearest to the Sun?

....

b)   Which planet has the most mass?

....

c)   Which planet has the least mass?

....

d)   Which planet takes the longest time to orbit the Sun?

....

e)   Complete the following sentence by circling the correct word.

The orbit time of planets *increases* / *decreases* as the distance from the Sun increases.

Q9   The asteroid belt lies between which two planets?

....

Q10   Which of the following objects are located in the Solar system? Circle the correct ones.

Stars   Comets   Asteroids   Galaxies   Planets   Moons

If you're stuck... see Page 97 of our KS3 Revision Guide (Levels 3-6) ☺

Types of Energy and Energy Transfer

Q1   The pictures below show examples of the eight main types of energy.

light,   kinetic,   sound,   elastic potential,
gravitational potential,   chemical,   electrical,   heat

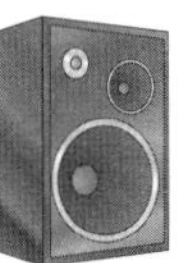

....

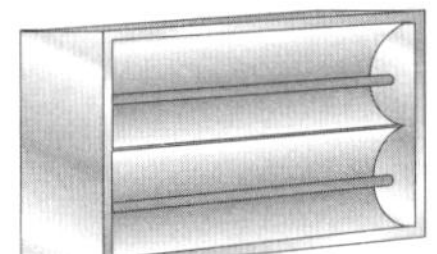

....

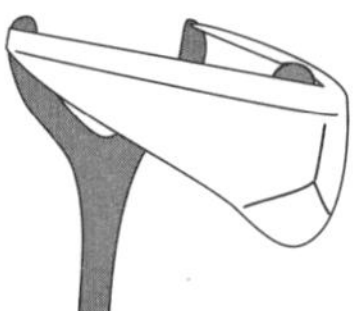

....

Q2

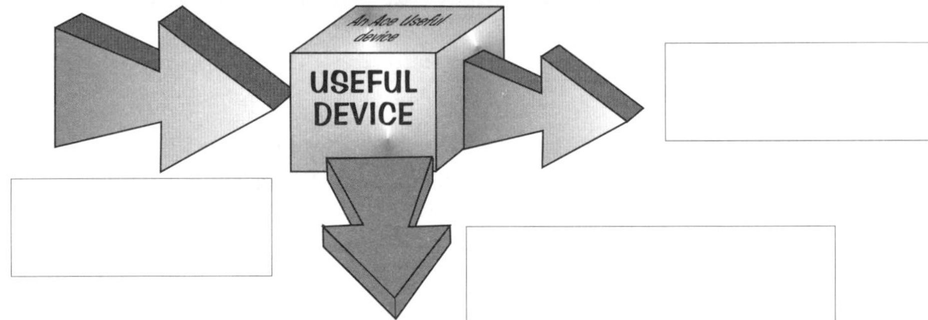

Is it possible to build a machine that doesn't waste any energy?

....

Energy Resources

The Sun is the source of most of the energy resources on the Earth.

Q1 Complete the energy diagrams below by writing the name of the final energy resource in the spaces provided. Use the words given in the grey box below.

> wave power,   wind power,   chemical (batteries),
> chemical (wood),   fossil fuel

a)

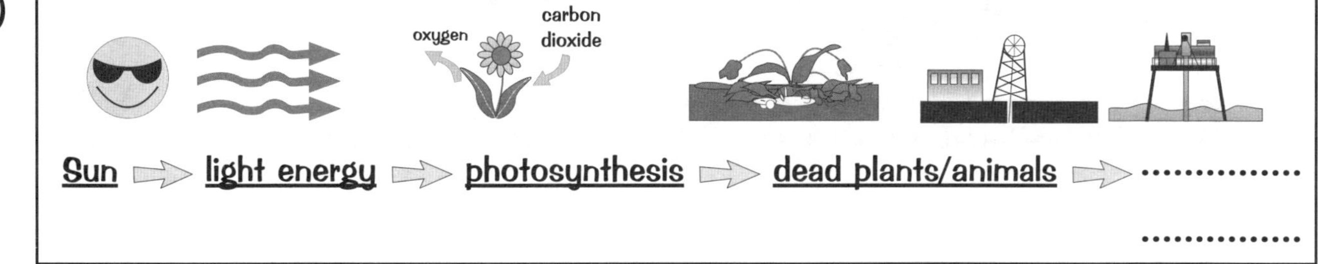

Sun ⇒ light energy ⇒ photosynthesis ⇒ dead plants/animals ⇒ ....
....

b)

Sun ⇒ heats atmosphere ⇒ causes winds ⇒ ....

c)

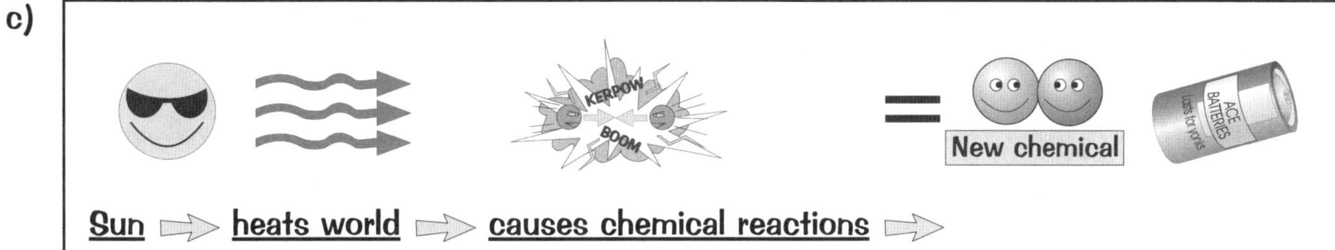

Sun ⇒ heats world ⇒ causes chemical reactions ⇒ ....

d)

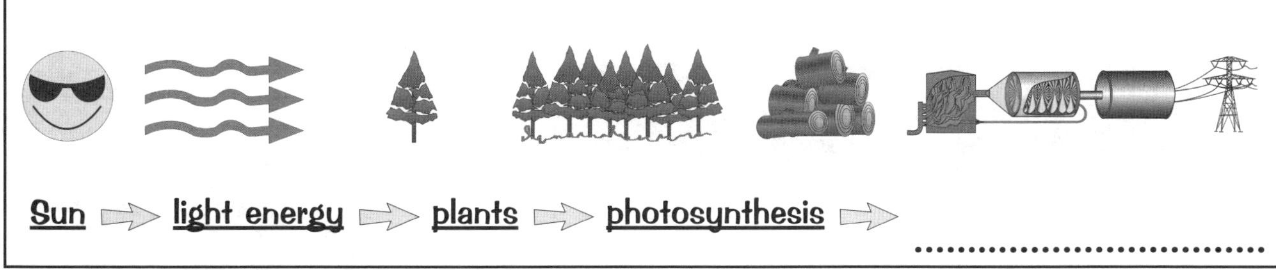

Sun ⇒ light energy ⇒ plants ⇒ photosynthesis ⇒ ....

e)

Sun ⇒ heats atmosphere ⇒ causes waves ⇒ ....

Generating Electricity

Q1 The diagram below shows how chemical energy can be converted to electrical energy.

a) **Name three types of fuel that can be used for the boiler.**

1) .... 2) .... 3) ....

b) **Are these energy sources "renewable" or "non-renewable"?**

1) .... 2) .... 3) ....

c) **Why isn't petrol burned in power stations?**

....

Q2 **Name two things people could do to help preserve non-renewable fuels.**

1) ....

2) ....

Q3 Other ways to produce electricity involve the use of renewable energy resources.
Most of these get their energy from the Sun.

Name the four forms of renewable energy shown in the three pictures.

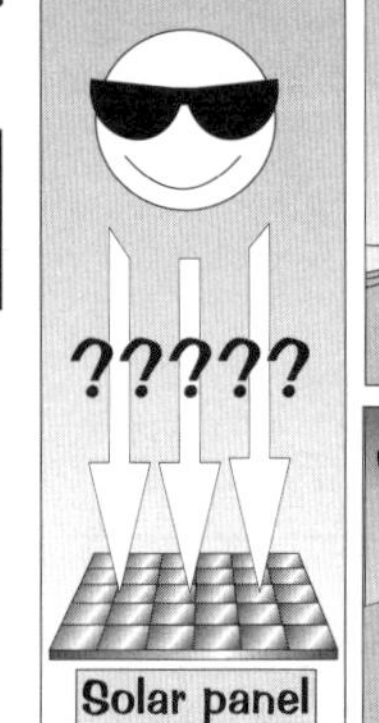
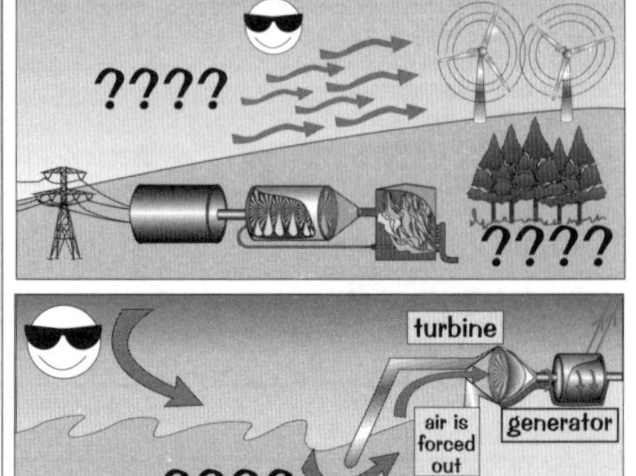

....

....

....

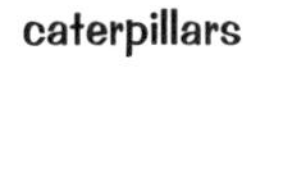

Q4 **Name a renewable energy resource that can be burnt.**

....